NEW MERMAIDS

General editor: Brian Gibbons
Professor of English Literature, University of Münster

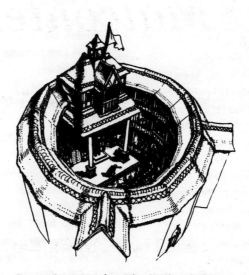

Reconstruction of an Elizabethan theatre
by C. Walter Hodges

John Marston

The Malcontent

with additions by John Webster

edited by W. David Kay

**Professor Emeritus of English
University of Illinois at Urbana-Champaign**

A & C Black • London

New Mermaids

3 5 7 9 10 8 6 4

Second edition 1998

Methuen Drama
A & C Black Publishers Limited
38 Soho Square
London W1D 3HB
www.acblack.com

ISBN: 978–07136–4288–9

First New Mermaid edition 1967
edited by Bernard Harris
published by Ernest Benn Limited
© 1967 Ernest Benn Limited

A CIP catalogue record for this book is available from the British Library

This book is produced using paper that is made from wood grown in
managed, sustainable forests. It is natural, renewable and recyclable.
The logging and manufacturing processes conform to the environmental
regulations of the country of origin.

Typeset in 9.5 on 10 pt Sabon by
Fakenham Photosetting Ltd, Fakenham, Norfolk

Printed in Great Britain by
CPI Cox & Wyman,
Reading, RG1 8EX

CONTENTS

To
Brian and Gordon

ACKNOWLEDGEMENTS

This revised edition of *The Malcontent* for the New Mermaid series necessarily draws on the researches of my predecessor, Bernard Harris, and on the contributions of other recent modern editors such as Macdonald Jackson and Michael Neill, Martin Wine, and G. K. Hunter, whose erudite Revels edition informs almost every page. Professor Hunter has graciously shared with me his correspondence with Alan Strachan and Jocelyn Powell. I am grateful to Oxford University Press for permission to reprint passages from Susan Snyder's edition of Sylvester's Du Bartas, and to the Nottingham Playhouse for permission to use photographs from its 1973 production. Christine Lodge of the Playhouse, Christopher Weir, Senior Archivist at the Nottinghamshire Archives, and Melanie Bachons of the Theatre Museum were most helpful in facilitating my theatre research; and the staffs of the Nottinghamshire Archives, the British Library, the Folger Shakespeare Library, and the Rare Book Room of the University of Illinois at Urbana-Champaign Library provided courteous and helpful assistance. As usual, Michael Shapiro has been an encouraging friend and has offered valuable comments about the Introduction. I wish to thank Anne Watts for her patience and efficiency, Brian Gibbons for being a most thorough and knowledgeable General Editor, and Sue Gibbons for her extremely attentive copy-editing. Their care in checking the text has saved me from many errors. For those that remain, I am responsible.

W. D. K.

ABBREVIATIONS

Editions of the Play Cited

Bullen	*John Marston: The Works*, ed. Arthur Henry Bullen, 3 vols. (1887, rpt. 1970), vol. 1
Dodsley	Robert Dodsley, *A Select Collection of Old Plays*, 3rd edition, ed. J. P. Collier, 12 vols. (1825–7), vol. 4
Dyce	*The Works of John Webster*, ed. Rev. Alexander Dyce, 2nd edition, 'Revised and Corrected' (1857)
Harris	*The Malcontent*, ed. Bernard Harris (The first New Mermaid edition) (1967)
Hunter	*The Malcontent*, ed. G. K. Hunter (The Revels Plays) (1975)
Jackson and Neill	*The Selected Plays of John Marston*, ed. Macdonald P. Jackson and Michael Neill (1986)
Wine	*The Malcontent*, ed. M. L. Wine (Regents Renaissance Drama series) (1964)
Wood	*The Plays of John Marston*, ed. H. Harvey Wood, 3 vols. (1934–9), vol. 1

Reference Works and Periodicals

ELR	*English Literary Renaissance*
ET	*The Elizabethan Theatre* (Waterloo, Ontario)
NQ	*Notes and Queries*
OED	*A New English Dictionary*, ed. J. A. Murray, H. Bradley, W. A. Craigie, and C. T. Onions, 13 vols. (1888–1933)
RD	*Renaissance Drama*
RES	*Review of English Studies*
SB	*Studies in Bibliography* (Virginia)
SEL	*Studies in English Literature*
SP	*Studies in Philology*
Tilley	M. P. Tilley, *A Dictionary of Proverbs in England in the Sixteenth and Seventeenth Centuries* (1950)

Shakespeare citations are to *The Riverside Shakespeare*, ed. G. Blakemore Evans (1974). Citations to Ben Jonson's plays are to *The Complete Plays of Ben Jonson*, ed. G. A. Wilkes, 4 vols. (1981). Citations to Greek and Latin poets are to the Loeb Classical Library. Quotations from Marston's *Certaine Satyres* and *The Scourge of Villanie* are from *The Poems of John Marston*, ed. Arnold Davenport (1961).

INTRODUCTION

The Play in Brief

A notable success when it was first performed, *The Malcontent* is a striking example of the new satiric tone and moral seriousness that distinguishes English comedy in the early 1600s. Patterned in part on Hamlet's 'antic disposition' and on Shakespeare's Thersites in *Troilus and Cressida*, its title character Malevole scathingly rebukes the lechery and self-seeking rampant in its courtly world, whose Genoese setting, like the Italian locales in the tragedies of Cyril Tourneur and John Webster, is a thin disguise for the Jacobean court and its vices. At the same time, the play's ironic intrigues issue not in bloody revenges but in moral transformations like those in Shakespeare's problem comedies and romances, where characters suffer from guilty intentions but not the achieved violence of tragedy that makes forgiveness and reconciliation impossible.

The happy ending of Marston's tragicomedy is dependent on the control over events allowed to Malevole, actually the deposed Duke Altofronto of Genoa in disguise. He remains at the court of the usurping Duke Pietro as a licensed critic, giving 'good intelligence' to Pietro's spirit by making him 'understand those weaknesses which others' flattery palliates' (I.ii.27–8). Using his blunt persona as a mask for intrigue, Altofronto initially attempts to destabilise the court by disclosing that Pietro has been cuckolded by the cunning villain Mendoza, whose interest in the Duchess Aurelia is motivated more by ambition than by love. Altofronto's plan is almost undone when the bawd Maquerelle, bribed with jewels, persuades Aurelia to reject Mendoza and begin an affair with the young courtier Ferneze. Confronted by Pietro, Mendoza protests his innocence and persuades Pietro to murder Ferneze, but in such a manner that Aurelia will think Mendoza the attempted protector of Ferneze rather than his killer. Mendoza's plot successfully reinstates him in Aurelia's favour, and together they agree to kill Pietro, who has foolishly made Mendoza his heir. Ironically, however, Mendoza recruits Malevole as the murderer, planning to report falsely that Pietro has committed suicide in grief over Aurelia's infidelity so that she can be banished. Instead of killing Pietro, Malevole reveals Mendoza's villainy to him, disguises him as the Hermit of the Rock, and brings him back to court, where he is given custody of Aurelia, now penitent and disillusioned by Mendoza's treachery. Mendoza, ignorant of their true identities, encourages Malevole and the Hermit to poison each other, intending then to marry Altofronto's duchess Maria when all his former accomplices have been killed or banished. His overconfident scheming, however, is undercut by Maria's defiant fidelity to Altofronto and by the audience's knowledge that Altofronto, Pietro, and the loyal Count Celso are working behind the scenes to defeat him. In the concluding masque devised to celebrate his installation as duke, Mendoza is surprised by force and contemptuously dismissed, Altofronto and Pietro are reunited with their wives, and Altofronto reassumes his title.

Marston's plot is full of amusing reversals and surprises, including four false deaths, two of which fool the audience as well as Mendoza. Incidental satire is provided by the figures of Maquerelle the bawd, Bilioso the time-serving court marshal, and the court ladies Emilia and Bianca, Bilioso's young wife. Webster's additions supplement the satire on them with amusing commentary by Passarello, a fool after the fashion of Shakespeare's Feste and Touchstone. These figures lighten the tone of the main action while re-enforcing its vision of a fallen humanity prone to lust and ambition. Despite Mendoza's villainy and Malevole's vivid attacks on vice, however, the reform of Pietro and Aurelia and the steadfast virtue of Maria, Celso, and Altofronto hold out some hope of social renewal at the play's end.

The Author

Marston's choice of an Italian setting (and, as we shall see, Italian literary sources) may have been influenced by his own heritage, for his mother, Mary Guarsi, was the daughter of an Italian surgeon resident in London. His father, also named John Marston, was a successful Coventry lawyer who served as a Reader at the Middle Temple in 1592. Marston was christened on 7 October 1576 in Wardington, Oxfordshire, matriculated at Brasenose College, Oxford, in 1592, and graduated B.A. in 1594. He had been admitted to the Middle Temple by virtue of his father's readership in 1592, and shared chambers there from 1595 to 1605. He apparently was more involved in the social and literary life of the Inns of Court than in legal studies, for his father's will, written on 24 October 1599 not long before his death, contains a cancelled passage expressing fear that his 'willfull disobedyent son' will sell his law books and complaining of 'his delighte in playes, vayne studies and fooleryes'.[1]

By 'fooleryes' his father no doubt referred to *The Metamorphosis of Pigmalions Image and Certaine Satyres* and *The Scourge of*

[1] Transcribed by David G. O'Neill, 'The Commencement of Marston's Career as a Dramatist', *RES*, 22 (1971), 444

Villanie, an Ovidian poem and two collections of verse satires published in 1598. These exhibit the same mixture of witty eroticism and satire on affected gallantry found in the works of other Inns of Court writers like the young John Donne, yet Marston's self-presentation as a scourger of vice is more extreme than Donne's urbane persona, and more contradictory. Alternating between righteous indignation and despair at the possibility of effecting meaningful reform, he contemptuously dismisses the effeminate fops, swaggering boasters, hypocritical Puritans, lustful sensualists, and courtly pretenders who parade across his satiric stage, but his own shifting postures – now a witty Ovidian and now an outraged Juvenalian, now the voice of 'grim Reproofe' and now of 'sporting merriment' – are not effectively managed. Despite his claim of moral intent, the Bishop of London and the Archbishop of Canterbury apparently found his Ovidian parody and his attacks on humours born in 'slime of filthy sensualitie' to be too vivid, for in June of 1599 they ordered his volumes to be publicly burnt along with nine offensive or subversive works by other writers.

Though Marston developed his skill at characterisation in verse satires, he was powerfully attracted to play-writing, confessing in the prefatory epistle to *The Fawn* that 'the over-vehement pursuit of these delights hath been the sickness of my youth'.[2] Our first evidence of his theatrical activity is the entry in Henslowe's *Diary* for 28 September 1599 of a payment of two pounds on behalf of the Admiral's Men to 'mr maxton the new poete' in earnest of an unspecified play, probably *Lust's Dominion, or The Lascivious Queen*, which seems to be identifiable with *The Spanish Moor's Tragedy* for which Henslowe made partial payment to Thomas Dekker, William Haughton, and John Day on 13 February 1599.[3] He also had a share in the anonymous estates morality play *Histriomastix, or The Player Whipt*, possibly written for the Middle Temple revels of 1598/99. All of the other plays identifiable as his were performed by the children's troupes, which specialised in satiric comedy and declamatory tragedy on Senecan themes. For the Children of Paul's he wrote *Antonio & Mellida* (1599), *Antonio's Revenge* (1600), *Jack Drum's Entertainment* (1600), and *What You Will* (1600–1), and he may have assisted Thomas Dekker in *Satiromastix, or the Untrussing of the Humorous Poet* (1601), the reply to Ben Jonson's *Poetaster* performed by both the Paul's boys and the Chamberlain's Men. For the Children of the Chapel Royal, known as the Children of the Queen's Revels after acquiring Queen Anne's patronage in February 1604, he wrote *The Malcontent*

---

[2] *The Fawn*, ed. Gerald A. Smith, Regents Renaissance Drama (1980), lines 11–12
[3] See Cyrus Hoy, *Introductions, Notes, and Commentaries to Texts in 'The Dramatic Works of Thomas Dekker'*, IV (1980), pp. 56–72

(1602–4), *Parasitaster, or The Fawn* (1604–6), *The Dutch Courtesan* (1604–5), *Eastward Ho* (with George Chapman and Ben Jonson, 1605), and *The Wonder of Women, or the Tragedy of Sophonisba* (1606). In 1606 he also composed some Latin verses for the entry of King Christian of Denmark into London and in 1607 *The Entertainment at Ashby* as a welcome for the Countess of Huntingdon's mother, the Dowager Countess of Derby. A final play, *The Insatiate Countess*, was published as his in 1613 but seems to have been left unfinished due to his imprisonment in 1608 and completed later by William Barksted and Lewis Machin.

Marston's difficulties with the authorities in 1608 were the culmination of a long history of literary quarrelsomeness and satire that exceeded allowable limits. Not only were his poems suppressed, but his sneers in *Certaine Satyres* at his fellow satirist Joseph Hall triggered a quarrel that was continued in *The Scourge of Villanie* and in epigrams, satires, and pamphlets issued from 1598 to 1601 by John Weever, Nicholas Breton, and Marston's cousin Everard Guilpin. With Ben Jonson he initiated the exchange of personal satire known as 'The War of the Theatres' for its broader involvement of the children's troupes and the adult companies in the years between 1599 and 1602. Jonson later reported that 'he had many quarrels with Marston, beat him, and took his pistol from him, wrote his *Poetaster* on him; the beginning of them were that Marston represented him in the stage'.[4] To his credit, Marston refined his poetic diction after Jonson satirised the awkwardness of his vocabulary in *Poetaster* (1601). Their reconciliation is evidenced by Marston's dedication of *The Malcontent* to him in 1604, his commendatory poem for Jonson's *Sejanus* (1605), and his collaboration with Jonson and Chapman on *Eastward Ho*. The latter, however, led to new difficulties because of its ridicule of King James and his Scots followers, of which Marston had also been guilty in *The Fawn* and *The Dutch Courtesan*. In this case he was forced to flee London to escape imprisonment with his collaborators, who were threatened with having their ears cropped and noses slit, the penalty for libel. Their indiscreet satire may, in a sense, have been encouraged by Queen Anne, for the French ambassador reported in June 1604 that she had attended plays representing James on stage 'in order to enjoy the laugh against her husband'.[5] But continuing offences resulted in the loss of the company's court patronage, and on 8 June 1608 Marston was committed to Newgate by the Privy Council, apparently for a play that

---

[4] *Conversations*, lines 282–5, in Jonson, *The Complete Poems*, ed. Parfitt, (rev. ed., 1988)

[5] Quoted by Linda Levy Peck, 'John Marston's *The Fawn*', in *The Theatrical City*, ed. David L. Smith and others (1995), p. 122

again ridiculed James, his favourites, and his questionable invest-
ments in Scottish silver mines.

This incident resulted in his forced retirement from the stage, and
Marston, always a moralist despite his lurid depiction of contemporary vice, turned to the church instead. At some time previously
he had married Mary Wilkes, daughter of Dr. William Wilkes, rector
of Barford St. Martin in Wiltshire and a chaplain to King James, and
in 1609 he returned to study at Oxford, where he was ordained
deacon by the Bishop of Oxford on 24 September and priest on 24
December. In 1610, when he was described in a lawsuit as 'John
Marston of Barford ... clerk', he was apparently serving as a curate
for his father-in-law, but on 10 October 1616 he became the incum-
bent of Christchurch, Hampshire. Since Wilkes' will, dated 6 May
1630, forgives him 'for lodging and diet, for himself, his wife, his
man, and mayde which he had of me for eleaven yeares',[6] he and
Mary had apparently been living with her father since 1605, which
gives point to Jonson's jest that 'Marston wrote his father-in-law's
preachings, and his father-in-law his comedies'.[7] Marston and his
wife had one son, who died in infancy in 1624. He resigned his living
on 13 September 1631, died on 25 June 1634, and was buried beside
his father in the choir of the Temple Church under a simple grave-
stone inscribed *Oblivioni Sacrum* ('Sacred to Oblivion'). The inscrip-
tion echoes the concluding poem 'To everlasting Oblivion' in *The
Scourge of Villanie*, which expresses his wish 'to sleepe secure, right
free from injurie / Of cancred hate, or rankest villanie'.[8] This youthful pose seems as much defiant as self-effacing, but his later renunci-
ation of fame was sincere, for in 1633, no doubt embarrassed to be
associated with the theatre after twenty-five years as a clergyman, he
requested that his name be removed from a collection of six of his
plays. Nevertheless, later students of Elizabethan drama have agreed
with William Camden's assessment of him, in *Remaines concerning
Britaine* (1605), as one of the 'most pregnant witts of these our
times, whom succeeding ages may justly admire'.[9]

The Play in Context

1. Dramatic auspices, date, publication, and additions

Initially the most popular of Marston's plays, *The Malcontent* was
first performed at the Blackfriars Theatre by the Children of the

---

[6] Quoted by R. E. Brettle, 'Notes on John Marston', *RES*, 13 (1962), 393
[7] *Conversations*, lines 198–99
[8] *Poems*, ed. Davenport, p. 175
[9] Quoted in *The Jonson Allusion-Book*, ed. Bradley and Adams (1922), p. 33

Chapel Royal / Queen's Revels. A product of the same disillusion-ment with the late Elizabethan and early Jacobean court that pro-duced Jonson's *Sejanus* and Chapman's *Bussy d'Ambois*, it was written sometime between 1602, the publication date of one of its sources, Dymock's translation of Guarini's *Il Pastor Fido* (*The Faithful Shepherd*), and 5 July 1604, when it was entered in the Stationers' Register. The allusion at I.viii.18–19 to a woman with a horn growing out of her forehead 'twelve years since' refers to the anonymous pamphlet, *A Miraculous and Monstrous Discourse*, published in 1588, but since this comes in one of the additions by John Webster (see below), it should probably be taken as a convenient round number, rather than as evidence the play was composed in 1600, when Marston was writing exclusively for the Children of Paul's. The slighting reference to 'Signior St. Andrew Jaques' at V.v.22 (apparently censored in the earliest editions) and the portrayal of Ferrardo as Pietro's male 'minion' would have more point after April or May of 1603, when the influx of Scots courtiers and King James' predilection for hand-some young men were becoming apparent, and a date of comple-tion later in that year seems most likely. However, since we know of nothing else written by Marston in 1602–3, it is possible he began the play earlier.

The Malcontent was printed in quarto in three different editions in 1604. The first two of these, referred to here as Q1 and Q2, pre-sent the text as performed at Blackfriars. The third (Q3) prints an expanded version played by Shakespeare's fellows at the Globe with additions by John Webster, known at this time primarily as Dekker's collaborator on historical plays for the adult troupes and on citizen comedies for the Children of Paul's. Described on the title-page as 'Augmented by Marston. / With the Additions played by the Kings Majesties servants. / Written by Jhon Webster', Q3 includes eleven new passages or scenes, as well as a clever 'Induction' by Webster that justifies the play's appropriation by the King's Men. In it, the actor Will Sly, in the character of a gallant, demands to know of the company's leaders 'how you came by this play?', to which Henry Condell, one of the sharers, replies:

> Faith, sir, the book was lost, and because 'twas pity so good a play should be lost, we found it and play it.
>
> SLY
>
> I wonder you would play it, another company having interest in it.
>
> CONDELL
>
> Why not Malevole in folio with us, as Jeronimo in decimo-sexto with them? They taught us a name for our play: we call it, *One for Another*.

SLY

    What are your additions?

BURBAGE

    Sooth, not greatly needful; only as your salad to your great feast, to entertain a little more time and to abridge the not-received custom of music in our theatre.   *(Induction* 73–83)

This passage raises several new questions, but makes three essential points: 1) the Blackfriars company had stolen one of the adult companies' plays about 'Jeronimo' – probably the anonymous *The First Part of Jeronimo*, a spin-off of Kyd's very popular *The Spanish Tragedy*; 2) the King's Men retaliated by performing *The Malcontent*, of which they had somehow obtained a copy; and 3) because it was written for the private theatre, in which a musical interlude was performed between each act, the play needed to be expanded to provide a proper afternoon's entertainment for the public theatre audience. (Q1 and 2 are, at some eighteen hundred and forty lines or so, shorter by one-fourth than the average public theatre play.) That the playbook really had been lost seems questionable, but whether Marston had already 'augmented' the text before the King's Men acquired their copy is unclear. If he had not done so, they would have needed his cooperation to revise it – a puzzling possibility in light of his continuing association with the Blackfriars troupe, unless the one-sixth share in the latter company he is said in a court suit to have held was subsequently offered to assure his continued writing for them.

When the King's Men obtained the play is also uncertain. The actor John Lowin, listed as playing in the Induction, did not join the company until after 12 March 1603, when he was still with Worcester's Men, but he became a member no later than early March of the following year, for he is included in the cast list for Jonson's *Sejanus*, performed before the end of 1603 (24 March 1604 in the old-style calendar). The play must have been performed frequently at the Blackfriars, for Sly says in Webster's Induction that he had seen the play 'often'. However, the theatres were closed because of the plague from mid-March 1603 until at least December, possibly even until the Lenten restrictions were lifted on 9 April 1604, though the Children of the Queen's Revels performed at court on 21 February 1604 (when a play about a virtuous duke defeating villainous 'policy' would certainly have been appropriate) and were said in a lawsuit to have performed fifteen weeks during the first year of James' reign.[10] If the play were written in late 1603 or early 1604, therefore, its production at the Blackfriars, acquisi-

---

[10] See Mark Eccles, 'Martin Peerson and the Blackfriars', *Shakespeare Survey*, 11 (1958)

tion by the King's Men, revision, and publication in three editions must have followed each other fairly closely, but since a work dated 1604 could have been printed anytime before 25 March 1605, there would have been sufficient time for the King's Men to revise it and to publish the third quarto. As in the case of the 1604 *Hamlet* quarto, they may have been willing to put their version in print promptly in order to stake their claim to it.

The eleven passages added in the play text proper fall mainly in the first and fifth acts. They are:

1) I.iii.106–47	7) V.i (complete)
2) I.iii.153–70	8) V.ii.9 s.d.–38
3) I.iv.43 s.d.–87 s.d.	9) V.iii.63 s.d.–94
4) I.viii (complete)	10) V.iv.17–30
5) II.iii.23–37	11) V.vi.133–54
6) III.i.32 s.d.–145	

Until recently, the discrepancy between the title-page's wording, with its implicit distinction between Marston's 'augmentations' and Webster's 'additions', and that of the heading to Sig. A3, which presents 'the Induction ... and the additions acted by the Kings Majesties servants' as written by Webster has long left commentators uncertain as to whether Marston wrote all of these eleven passages or none of them. However, the analysis of their style and function by G. K. Hunter, supported by the linguistic analysis of D. J. Lake, has established with some certainty that Marston is responsible for numbers 1, 2, 3, 5, 9 and 11, which expand Malevole's speeches and emphasise the opportunism of Bilioso.[11] The others, which feature comic dialogue involving some combination of the court fool Passarello (added in Q3), Malevole, Bilioso, or Bilioso's witty wife Bianca, use linguistic patterns characteristic of Webster. Webster's additions impede the movement of the plot somewhat, but they are full of amusing satiric touches. Moreover, two of the added scenes (I.viii and V.i) were structurally necessary at the Globe, where musical interludes between acts were not customary as at the Blackfriars, for they prevent the exit and immediate re-entry of characters in violation of the public theatre's conventions of continuous staging. They are printed here as they were in Q3 so that readers can experience the play as it was adapted by Shakespeare's company without having to turn back and forth to an appendix. Those who wish to focus on Marston's leaner version should begin with the Prologue and skip over those sections marked as Webster's in the notes.

---

[11] Hunter, Revels edition, pp. xlvi–liii, and D. J. Lake, 'Webster's Additions to *The Malcontent*', *NQ*, April, 1981

2. Dramatic mode

Marston's text was entered in the Stationer's Register as 'An Enterlude called *the Malecontent Tragiecomedia*', evidence that at some level Marston conceived his play to be an innovation in literary form, and it has generally been assumed that he was copying Italian models. Though English playwrights had created double-plot plays contrasting happy and sad endings or comedies containing deaths among the minor characters, such as Heywood's *A Woman Killed with Kindness* or Greene's *Friar Bacon and Friar Bungay*, they had been less concerned to defend their practice than Italian poets and critics. A 'mixed' form of Senecan-inspired tragedy that combined deaths for the evil characters and a happy ending for the good ones had been advocated in 1543 by Giovanbattista Giraldi Cinthio, whose dramatisation of the virtues of clemency in rulers and fidelity in wives parallels *The Malcontent*'s themes and whose play *Selene* offers inexact, but suggestive analogies to the schemes of Marston's Mendoza.[12] A more definite source of Marston's inspiration is Giambattista Guarini's *Il Pastor Fido* (*The Faithful Shepherd*) a tale of lovers separated by ambiguous oracles and the machinations of the jealous Corisca, the heroine's rival. From its 1602 English translation Marston drew some of the wording for Ferneze's wooing of Aurelia, for Maquerelle's cynical advice to her female disciples, and for Mendoza's Machiavellian principles. Moreover, his careful balancing of tragic and comic elements seems to match that recommended in Guarini's *Il Compendio della Poesia Tragicomica* (1601), a combination of two earlier defences of *Il Pastor Fido*. Implicitly disagreeing with Giraldi's view that deaths were allowable in tragicomedy, Guarini defines it not as a mixture of comic and tragic outcomes but as a judicious selection of features from each of the two modes:

> He who composes tragicomedy takes from tragedy its great persons but not its great action, its verisimilar plot but not its true one, its movement of the feelings but not its disturbance of them, its pleasure but not its sadness, its danger but not its death; from comedy it takes laughter that is not excessive, modest amusement, feigned difficulty, happy reversal, and above all the comic order.[13]

---

[12] Noted by Bernard Harris in the first New Mermaid edition, p. xxvii: 'There the villain, Gripo, secretary to the Queen, informs King Rodobano, falsely, of his wife's infidelity, arranges an ambush in which he intends to kill the King, and turns his subsequent failure to do so into an advantage by pretending that he has saved the Queen from her husband's assault'

[13] Guarini, *Il Compendio della Poesia Tragicomica* (1601), trans. Alan H. Gilbert, *Literary Criticism: Plato to Dryden* (1962), p. 511. For Guarini's influence, see Arthur C. Kirsch, *Jacobean Dramatic Perspectives* (1972), and G. K. Hunter, 'Italian Tragicomedy on the English Stage', *RD*, n.s. 6 (1973)

Although Marston's bawdy jesting hardly qualifies as 'modest amusement' and although he avoids Sophoclean discoveries of identity like those which produce the last-minute 'happy reversal' in the fortunes of Guarini's pastoral lovers, his story of usurping dukes, his control of the audience's emotional engagement, and his contrivance of a purely comic ending fulfill Guarini's prescriptions. Moreover, in the context of the early Jacobean court, where Queen Anne and leading ladies of her household like Lady Bedford patronised the Italian humanist John Florio and participated in masques modelled on Italian entertainments, his borrowings from Guarini and the echoes of Tasso and Ariosto in Pietro's narrative of his supposed suicide (see notes to IV.iii) may have functioned as intertextual allusions that flattered the sophistication of auditors capable of recognising them. Only a year later in *Volpone*, Jonson satirises the fashionable enthusiasm for Italian culture when he has the pretentious Lady Would-be rattle off a catalogue of her favourite Italian poets and seize enthusiastically on *Il Pastor Fido*, exclaiming, 'all our English writers ... such as are happy in the Italian / Will deign to steal out of this author [Guarini] mainly' (III.iv.87–92).

At the same time, Marston's handling of tone and plot make *The Malcontent* quite different from that of *Selene* and *Il Pastor Fido*, and we must be careful not to overstate his indebtedness to Italian tragicomedy. His play is far less static and melodramatic than Giraldi's, which sentimentally plays up Selene's emotional distress at her husband's mistaken suspicions and her long separation from him in order to emphasise the poetic justice of the villain Gripo's execution and Selene's restoration to happiness. It is also quite different in spirit from Guarini's pastoral, with its woodland setting, romantic lyrics, priests and oracles, and neo-classical choruses. Marston's real achievement in *The Malcontent*, in fact, is to assimilate his Italian and classical sources into patterns of English dramatic satire and native revenge tragedy, putting to more effective use motifs that he had used less satisfactorily earlier. As dramatic satire, his presentation of Malevole-Altofronto resolves many of the tensions evident in the literary personae of his early works while gripping the audience's attention with a scathing assault on flattery, ambition, and lust. As a comical variation on revenge tragedy, his plot retains the dark ironies of Machiavellian intrigue while minimising sensational violence and producing a 'clean' revenger who is the agent of social and moral reform. The result is a happy combination of ironic plotting, satiric characterisation, biting social commentary, and moral reflection that is uniquely Marston's own.

3. Malevole as malcontent and satirist

As a satiric agent Malevole attacks vice with the vigour of W.

Kinsayder, the 'barking Satyrist' of Marston's verse satires, but his
true identity as the banished Duke Altofronto tempers the extrem-
ism of the satiric role and motivates his violent assault on hypocrisy
and deceit.[14] Seeking with Hercules 'to purge the world from muck',
Kinsayder had often seemed to wallow in it, and in the 'Satyra
Nova' added to the second edition of *The Scourge of Villanie*
Marston had questioned whether he was not 'frantique, foolish,
bedlam mad' to waste his spirit by playing 'the rough part of a
Satyrist' for an audience of 'dung-scum rable'.[15] Marston's early
attempts to incorporate the satirist into a dramatic setting awk-
wardly expose these contradictions: in *Antonio and Mellida* the
claims of the blunt commentator Feliche to contentment at his low
position (his name means 'fortunate' or 'happy') seem belied by the
violence of his reaction to figures like the flatterer Forobosco:

> O how I hate that same Egyptian louse,
> A rotten maggot, that lives by stinking filth
> Of tainted spirits. Vengeance to such dogs
> That sprout by gnawing senseless carrion!
>
> (*Antonio and Mellida* II.i.149–52)[16]

Marston is careful to present Feliche's anger as righteous indignation, directed not at individual men, but at 'man's lewd qualities'
(III.ii.305), yet Feliche's moral outrage seems inconsistent with his
pose as a Stoic wise man. However, in *The Malcontent*,
Altofronto's anger is a justifiable reaction caused by his bitter
experience with political duplicity. Like Prospero in Shakespeare's
The Tempest, who is undoubtedly modelled on him, Altofronto
lacked 'those old instruments of state, / Dissemblance and suspect'
and 'so slept in fearless virtue, / Suspectless, too suspectless' till a
popular alliance with Florence, engineered by Mendoza and Pietro,
deprived him of his dukedom (I.iv.9–17). Though his goals at the
beginning of the play are not entirely clear, the soliloquy added to
the end of I.iii in Q3 emphasises the justness of his revenge, which,
like the 'inward pinches' Prospero inflicts on his noble antagonists,
is aimed at Pietro's soul. At the same time, the 'affected strain' he
adopts as his verbal disguise, like Hamlet's 'antic disposition', func-
tions both as a role behind which he can hide and as an outlet for
deeply-felt exasperation at the world's corruption.
  In assuming the guise of a malcontent, Altofronto was playing a
role that would have been familiar to Marston's contemporaries
from both literature and life. The universities of Elizabethan

---

[14] See Bridget Gellert Lyons, *Voices of Melancholy* (1971), pp. 58–76
[15] *Poems*, pp. 149, 163
[16] References to the *Antonio* plays are to *Selected Plays*, ed. Jackson and Neill (1986)

England graduated more young men than could find positions in church and state, and disaffection was increased by the age's religious conflicts and by Elizabeth's reluctance to distribute honours among the younger generation of the gentry and aristocracy. In the Essex conspiracy of 1601 such disaffection had turned into outright rebellion, but it had been given literary recognition since the late 1580s by allusions to malcontents in Elizabethan fiction and prose satire. Thomas Lodge offers a typical portrait in *Wits Miserie, and the Worlds Madnesse: Discovering the Devils Incarnat of this Age*, where the compound figure of Scandal and Detraction is described as 'a right malecontent Devill' who skulks in the back aisles of Paul's, 'his lookes suspitious and heavie'. A traveller corrupted by foreign vices, he is an atheist or counterfeit Catholic who has read Machiavelli and 'delighteth in nought els but traiterous and devillish stratagems'.[17] Lodge's equation of alienation and villainy is echoed by Lussurioso in *The Revenger's Tragedy*, who recruits Vindice to do his dirty work on the assumption that 'discontent and want / Is the best clay to mold a villain of' (IV.i.48–9). Ironically, both Lussurioso and Marston's Mendoza are deceived by Vindice's and Malevole's malcontented poses and so undone, but in Webster's *The Duchess of Malfi* and *The White Devil* the malcontents Bosola and Flamineo come to tragic ends when they allow themselves to be used as the tools of corrupt noblemen.

Marston's Malevole may have been the inspiration for these tragic malcontents, but he is first and foremost a blunt critic rather than a knavish rogue. Early hints for his name and function can be found in Marston's *Certaine Satyres*, where the exhausted satirist proposes to abandon the role of 'malevolent' beadle (or whipper) 'to the world's impuritie' (V.175–6), and in *Antonio's Revenge*, where Alberto urges Antonio not to disguise himself as a fool, but rather to 'put on some trans-shaped cavalier, / Some habit of a spitting critic' (IV.i.3–4). As an open railer against courtly vice, Malevole is also modelled on Thersites in *Troilus and Cressida* and on the figure of Diogenes the Cynic, depicted as a bold censurer of kings and counsellors in John Lyly's *Campaspe* and in Lodge's *Catharos: Diogenes in his Singularitie* (1591). Malevole's links to 'the currish mad *Athenian*', as Marston calls Diogenes in *The Scourge of Villanie* VII, are emphasised by the canine imagery at I.ii.9–11, and illustrated by his snarling attack on the court in the play's dramatic opening. His scatological and animal metaphors expose the corruption and beastliness of Pietro's courtiers, condemning Ferrardo as a ferret or weasel for his lecherous predations, Prepasso as an ape for his courtly ceremony, and Bilioso as a 'muckhill overspread with fresh snow' for his hypocritical flattery. His

[17] Thomas Lodge, *Works*, ed. Gosse (1883), IV, pp. 23–24

attack on this fallen world is sustained brilliantly by a variety of rhetorical strategies – direct vituperation, riddling allusions and metaphors, ironic catalogues, and vivid descriptions that gain credibility from the play's action. So his satiric dream-vision at I.iii.47–54 of a pleasure-seeking society of jewelled panders and adulterous lords and ladies anticipates Ferneze's bribery of the bawd Maquerelle to advance him in Aurelia's favour, and it is later re-enforced by his graphic warning to Bilioso at III.ii.24–50 of the seductive allurements to which his wife will be subject in 'an Italian lascivious palace', where 'sweet music, amorous masquerers, / Lascivious banquets' and 'that great bawd, Opportunity' would tempt even Penelope in Homer's *Odyssey* to commit adultery. With Mendoza, on the other hand, he assumes a saucy familiarity – jesting, inventing zany similes, matching Machiavellian sentences, and endorsing or elaborating Mendoza's villainous plots with parodic enthusiasm.

4. Altofronto as an agent of reform

Altofronto's malcontent persona is so vivid, in fact, that his ducal self has been harder to define, and G. K. Hunter has complained that 'there is really no Altofront language to provide an alternative vision to that of Malevole'.[18] That Marston intended some formal distinction between his two roles may be seen from the stage direction at I.iv.43, which reads, 'BILIOSO *entering* MALEVOLE *shifteth his speech*', indicating a change from blank verse to prose and perhaps also to a more 'antic' mode of speaking. On a more fundamental level, however, Altofronto is sustained by the quiet faith that there is a rational world-order amenable to virtue, despite the corruption and depravity on which he harps as Malevole. Keenly aware of the vicissitudes of Fortune from having lost his 'state', he ultimately sees Fortune as subservient to Providence, while trusting that evil will defeat itself through its own internal divisions and excessive greed. In his persona as a malcontent Altofronto continually reminds Mendoza that knavish villains rise only to fall, as in his fable at II.iii.18–22 of the ambitious tortoise who is taken aloft by eagles and then dropped from a great height. In his own person, however, he takes a Stoical view of his own dethroning as a fall from which he can only rise. Affirming that '*He's resolute who can no lower sink*' (I.iv.43), he sows division between Pietro and Mendoza with the aim of creating opportunities for intervention: 'Discord to malcontents is very manna; / When the ranks are burst, then scuffle Altofront' (ll. 38–9). Yet as Robert Beale Bennett points out, his hope is 'grounded in the belief that evil governance will

---

inevitably descend into chaos'.[19] In contrast to Celso, who wishes to 'mutiny and die' in a futile romantic gesture, Altofronto chooses to 'temporise' (ll. 25–8). Though he has earlier admitted his inability to 'time it' by dissembling (l. 10), he does not seem to use 'temporise' here or at IV.v.144 in the sense of compromising one's principles to fit the time and circumstances (*OED* 1), but in the sense of delaying or waiting for a more favourable moment (*OED* 2).[20] The wise passivity he advocates, however, involves a shrewd alertness to the plots of others rather than constant machinations of his own, and it does not take much plotting to bring Mendoza down. Confirming Altofronto's conviction that *'Envious Ambition never sates his thirst, / Till sucking all, he swells, and swells, and bursts'* (I.iv.78–9), Mendoza's own scheming gradually unites the court and the Florentine powers against him, and in his overconfidence he himself suggests the fable for the masque that will bring his enemies together disguised as 'brave spirits of the Genoan dukes'. Though Altofronto devises the fiction that Pietro killed himself in grief over Aurelia's infidelity, his primary tasks are to preserve Mendoza's victims and to lead them to repentance, just as Duke Vincentio in *Measure for Measure* prevents Angelo from harming others and engineers his public exposure and penance.

With Aurelia, Altofronto works through Pietro in his role as Hermit of the Rock. Pietro's moving description of his supposed suicide and the shock of Mendoza's sudden abandonment jolt her out of her 'blushless impudence', leaving her 'worthily most miserable'. Though Pietro is presented to her in disguise as a spiritual counsellor, he is more a sympathetic witness of her suffering than an active agent of her redemption, for she has already come to realize the difference between a true husband and false lover, so recalling the argument that Hamlet must impress on Gertrude. When Pietro asks, 'Belike your lord not loved you, was unkind?', she replies:

> Oh heaven!
> As the soul loved the body, so loved he;
> 'Twas death to him to part my presence,
> Heaven to see me pleased.
> Yet I, like to a wretch given o'er to hell,
> Brake all the sacred rites of marriage,

---

[19] Robert Beale Bennett, *Medieval and Renaissance Drama in England*, 1 (1984), p. 76

[20] The view of Altofronto as a Machiavellian has been propounded by Philip J. Finkelpearl, *John Marston of the Middle Temple* (1969); T. F. Wharton, 'The *Malcontent* and "Dreams, Visions, Fantasies" ', *Essays in Criticism*, 24 (1974); and Lloyd Davis, *Guise and Disguise* (1993)

> To clip a base, ungentle, faithless villain,
> Oh God, a very pagan reprobate! –
> What should I say? – Ungrateful, throws me out,
> For whom I lost soul, body, fame, and honour.
> But 'tis most fit: why should a better fate
> Attend on any who forsake chaste sheets,
> Fly the embrace of a devoted heart,
> (Joined by a solemn vow 'fore God and man)
> To taste the brackish blood of beastly lust
> In an adulterous touch?   (IV.v.31–46)

Marston's poetry here is a remarkable bit of creative imitation, for it echoes both Hamlet's pained recollection in I.ii of his father's devotion to Gertrude and his indignant attack in III.iv on his mother's lovemaking 'in the rank sweat of an enseamed bed' with 'a slave that is not twentieth part the tithe / Of your precedent lord' and yet retains some freshness. Aurelia, however, proves her penitence by needing no external condemnation to stimulate her remorse. Her tears of regret in this scene prepare for her tears of joy at her reconciliation with Pietro in the end.

Pietro's willingness to give Malevole 'free liberty' bodes well for his own spiritual potential, and Altofronto works more directly with him, playing the sharp surgeon by taunting Pietro with his title of 'Duke' and his status as a cuckold. Initially, he seems to encourage Pietro to murder Mendoza (see I.iii.145–9), but 'the too-soft Duke' is easily dissuaded from this purpose by Mendoza's false protestations of loyalty. As Mendoza's plots unfold, Altofronto's strategy changes to disillusioning Pietro about his villainy. His *contemptus mundi* speeches only confirm Pietro's own experience with fallen humanity as demonstrated by Aurelia's lust, Mendoza's deceit, and Bilioso's unprincipled time-serving, all of which are painfully revisited immediately before his conversion in IV.v. Pietro's response focuses on the retribution he has incurred for his own treachery:

> Oh Altofront, I wrong thee to supplant thy right,
> To trip thy heels up with a devilish sleight,
> For which I now from throne am thrown; world-tricks abjure,
> For *vengeance, though't comes slow, yet it comes sure.*
> Oh, I am changed, for here, 'fore the dread power,
> In true contrition I do dedicate
> My breath to solitary holiness,
> My lips to prayer, and my breast's care shall be
> Restoring Altofront to regency.   (IV.v. 120–8)

These remarks are the product of independent moral reflection, and like Aurelia's acceptance of punishment and desire for reconciliation, his willingness to work for Altofronto's restoration is evidence, as William W. E. Slights notes, that he is penitent enough to make satisfaction for his wrong-doing.[21]

Is Altofronto's rhetoric self-justifying? Pietro's speech is important evidence to the contrary. First, it establishes that Altofronto's assumption of 'right' at the end of the play is recognised as rightful by others and is not just another persona adopted to mask the legitimation of power. Q3's addition to Altofronto's last speeches, in fact, specifically warns against mistaking a magisterial demeanour or ceremonial pomp for real government. '[F]aces / And outward shows' may mislead 'th'inconstant people', but true authority is derived only from virtuous rule. '[G]reat ones' are reminded that 'When they observe not Heaven's imposed conditions, / They are no kings, but forfeit their commissions' (V.vi.139–45). This statement is more a prophetic warning than a fully worked-out political theory, for the play both accepts, with Pietro, the concept of legitimate succession and yet makes the ruler's legitimacy contingent on his obedience to divine precept. The Jacobean censors were troubled enough by its implications to insist on changing 'kings' to 'men'.

Secondly, along with Aurelia's belief that Mendoza 'shall not miss sad punishment / 'Fore he shall rule' (IV.v.10–11), Pietro's submission to 'the dread power' extends the affirmation of divine retribution and Providential intervention into a general principle in this dramatic world, thereby validating Altofronto's own interpretation of his conversion:

> Who doubts of Providence,
> That sees this change, a hearty faith to all?
> *He needs must rise who can no lower fall,*
> For still impetuous vicissitude
> Touseth the world; then let no maze intrude
> Upon your spirits; wonder not I rise,
> *For who can sink that close can temporise?*   (IV.v. 138–44)

Some critics have found the shifts in Altofronto's thinking to be contradictory, but the underlying coherence of his thought comes clear in the context of the whole scene and his affirmations throughout the play. He, Pietro, Ferneze, and Celso must unite to 'stand / Full shock of Fortune' (ll. 131–2), but they can do so with trust in Providence and confidence that their fortunes will improve if they patiently bide their time in secrecy. For, as Altofronto puts it a bit later, '*no disastrous chance can ever move him / That feareth nothing but a God above him*' (V.iv.90–1).[22]

---

[21] See William W. E. Slights, ' "Elder in a deform'd church" ', *SEL*, 13 (1973)
[22] For views of Fortune and Providence in the play, see Geoffrey Aggeler, 'Stoicism

5. Mendoza and Machiavellian villainy

Altofronto's main antagonist and the worldling whom Fortune 'touses' most is, of course, Mendoza, whose ambition is the engine that drives Marston's plot. Aiming to seize and consolidate power by seduction, murder, and politically-motivated marriage, he is in many ways reminiscent of Piero, Duke of Venice in *Antonio's Revenge*, but his ancestry is complex.[23] Not so much a realistic study in the Tacitean arts of government practised in contemporary Italy as a caricature of the 'politic' villain, Mendoza is compounded from the Elizabethan stage-Machiavel and the tyrants of Seneca's tragedies. A popular dramatic sub-genre of the 1580s and '90s was the villain-hero play, in which an unprincipled, self-seeking climber spins out overly-elaborate plots, only to be caught at last in the toils of his own wit. Usually depicted as a foreigner or exotic alien, the stage-Machiavel uses his 'winding wit' to fool an extensive series of victims, killing off those who block his upward path as well as his accomplices, often by poison. Blinded by overconfidence, he is undone in turn by an ironic plot, leaving the audience pleased at his downfall, which is presented less as tragedy than as black comedy. The original pattern for these villain-hero plays was Marlowe's *The Jew of Malta*, where Barabas is introduced to the audience by Machiavelli himself. Marlowe's work inspired a host of imitations, and *The Malcontent* is indebted rather directly to several of them, notably *Lust's Dominion*, where the Moorish Eleazar's betrayal of the Spanish Queen Mother parallels Mendoza's perfidy

---

and Revenge in Marston', *English Studies* (1970), and George L. Geckle, *John Marston's Drama* (1980)

[23] Like Piero, who is modelled in part on the exploits of Francesco and Galeazzo Maria Sforza, he evokes the ruthless drive for power and the amoral cunning of the fifteenth- and early sixteenth-century Italian princes chronicled in Machiavelli's *The Prince* and Guicciardini's *History of Italy*, which was available to Marston in Geoffrey Fenton's 1599 translation with side-notes that called attention to 'dissimulations', 'suttleties', or 'politike dealing'. From William Thomas' *The Historie of Italie* (1549), Marston may have learned that Genoa, where *The Malcontent* is set, had a reputation for political instability and frequent changes of its dukes, but his depiction of Florence as its overlord is unhistorical and may be due to Florence's association with 'Machiavellian' strategy, for he grounds Aurelia's brazenness in her overconfidence in her Medici connections (see II.v.79–81). Yet curiously, there is little else to connect the court world depicted in *The Malcontent* specifically to Italy, aside from that country's image in the popular imagination (fed by such Protestant propaganda as Innocent Gentillet's treatise *Contre-Machiavell*) as a land of intrigue, poison, and political treachery. See G. K. Hunter, 'English Folly and Italian Vice', in *Jacobean Theatre*, ed. J. R. Brown and B. Harris (1960), and Mario Praz, 'Machiavelli and the Elizabethans', *The Flaming Heart* (1958)

to Aurelia,[24] and *Alphonsus, Emperor of Germany*, where Alphonsus' poisoning of Lorenzo de Cyprus parallels Mendoza's attempt to eliminate Malevole.[25] In line with his portrayal of Mendoza as a comical villain, however, Marston gives an ironic twist to the convention, making Malevole anticipate Mendoza's treachery and only pretend to be poisoned.

As active intriguers, Elizabethan stage-Machiavels continue the English stage tradition of cunning deception initiated by the morality play Vice, but their tendency to rationalise their villainy with maxims extolling fraud or force links them with the Senecan tyrant. If Machiavellianism and Stoicism confront each other as 'mighty opposites' in Elizabethan drama, it is because they had already been similarly contrasted in the tragedies of Seneca, where cruel rulers who glory in their power are opposed by victims whose resolution is steeled by contempt of Fortune.[26] In *The Malcontent*, thankfully, Marston abandons such outward trappings of Senecan tragedy as the ghosts, the forebodings, the exaggerated rhetoric and bloody stage business he had employed in *Antonio's Revenge*, but he retains Seneca's dense sententiousness, indicated in the original quartos by italics or inverted commas that signal notable aphorisms. Interestingly, many of the 'Machiavellian' maxims spoken by Mendoza, such as '*Mischief that prospers men do virtue call*' and '*Who cannot bear with spite, he cannot rule*' (V.iv.75, 79), are not derived from Machiavelli at all, but are adapted from Seneca; at times Mendoza even quotes him directly, as does Malevole when he wants to display his knavish credentials (see II.i.26 and V.iv.14). On the other hand, Altofronto, as we have seen, counters these maxims with other Senecan 'sentences' about Providential intervention and the eventual change of Fortune for the better.

Marston's attention to balance and his careful control of tone are major means by which he sustains his plot's comic potential. Though Mendoza has many of the characteristics of a true Machiavellian villain like Shakespeare's Edmund or Iago, he is exaggerated just enough to make him slightly ridiculous. A prime example of his absurdity is his day-dream of a favourite's power, in which he imagines 'a confused hum and busy murmur of obsequious suitors training him ... petitionary vassals licking the pavement with their slavish knees, whilst some odd palace-lamprels that engender with snakes and are full of eyes on both sides, with a kind of insinuated humbleness, fix all their delights upon his brow' (I.v.25–31). His vision of courtly greatness is such an unrealistically

---

[24] See above, p. xi and n. 3

[25] See F. T. Bowers, 'The Date and Composition of *Alphonsus, Emperor of Germany*', *Harvard Studies ... in Philology and Literature*, 15 (1933)

[26] See the essay by Joseph S. M. J. Chang in *RD*, 9 (1966), and Praz, *op. cit.*

self-aggrandising fantasy that it is not surprising to hear him ask when he is finally cornered by his opponents, 'Do I dream? Or have I dreamt / This two days' space?' (V.vi.114–15). Essentially, he is presented as a comic humour, allowed for a time to swell with pride in 'prosperous treachery' but ultimately deflated by the ironies of Altofronto's counter-plotting, exposed, and driven out.

6. Other contrasting pairs

Other paired contrasts help to order the play's structure, extending Marston's satire while dramatising the moral norms against which vice is judged, norms that are not simply derived from a 'mythical past' but are actively demonstrated in the play's present. Bilioso, the time-serving courtier who would rather 'stand with wrong, than fall with right' (IV.v.90) is contrasted with Celso, the 'constant lord' who is free from 'shifting cowardice / And fearful baseness' (III.iii.15–16). Maquerelle, Emilia, and Bianca, who illustrate the licentiousness of a court where fidelity to one's spouse is subordinate to profit and pleasure, are counterbalanced by the chaste Maria and the penitent Aurelia. In the 'augmentations' to I.iv and V.iii Marston expands Bilioso's role in order to illustrate more fully how his attitude toward Malevole shifts with the wind of court favour, showing him to be so eager to ingratiate himself with those in power that he offers the sexual services of his wife and daughter-in-law. These additions make his role more equal to that of Maquerelle, who is one of Marston's most successful comic creations. A lively variation on the conventional figure of the experienced courtesan or woman of the world, such as Scapha in Plautus' *The Haunted House* or Corisca in *Il Pastor Fido*, she offers the younger women in the court cynical advice on how to use cosmetics, hide their infidelities, and manipulate and exploit men. In her role as bawd and provider of aphrodisiacs like the 'restorative posset' enjoyed in II.iv, she satirises the courtly underworld that ministered to the lust of the Jacobean nobility, prefiguring the notorious Mistress Anne Turner who aided Frances Howard's intrigue with Robert Carr, Earl of Somerset, just a few years later.[27] As an unrepentant sensualist and expert in controlling men,

---

[27] Married at age twelve to the Earl of Essex, whom she loathed, Frances Howard divorced him on the grounds of impotence and married Carr with the King's support. Mistress Turner assisted her in obtaining love potions for Somerset, medicine to keep Essex impotent, and poison to murder Carr's secretary Sir Thomas Overbury, who opposed the match. For a narrative account see G. P. V. Akrigg, *Jacobean Pageant: the Court of King James I* (1962), pp. 177–204; David Lindley's *The Trials of Frances Howard* (1993) offers a sympathetic defence of Lady Frances as a victim of contemporary misogyny.

reminiscent of the Wife of Bath, she may seem to represent a mis-
ogynistic strain in Marston's satire. However, as with Mendoza's
contrasting praise and dispraise of women (see I.v and I.vi),
Marston treats her vices as part of the play's dialectic, balancing her
comical enthusiasm for 'the falling fashion' against Maria's resolute
chastity and fidelity to Altofronto, which is tested in Act V after the
fashion of Boccaccio's Griselda and Seneca's heroines. Maquerelle
and Bilioso may be more vivid than their opposites, but Maria,
Celso, and the Captain of the Citadel stand as admirable represen-
tatives of virtuous constancy in a morally corrupted society. They
form the core of the new social order in a reformed Genoa and are
rewarded in the play's closing moments by Altofronto's embraces,
while Bilioso and Maquerelle are rebuked.

7. The ending

The faith that justice, virtue, and marital fidelity can triumph over
Machiavellian self-seeking, flattery, and lustful pleasure was badly
needed in the early seventeenth century and still is today. Marston
was no doubt aware that affirming such a faith is difficult, for he
makes Altofronto's restoration dependent on the surprisingly moral
response to the disordered Genoan court by its Florentine overlord,
and he does not pretend that figures like Ferneze can be completely
reformed. Nevertheless, the fiction of a virtuous ruler shrewd
enough to battle corruption and unmask deceptive evil is an appeal-
ing fantasy. Shakespeare returned to it twice in *Measure for
Measure* and *The Tempest*, making the spiritual transformation
wrought in Aurelia and Pietro by Altofronto the pattern for the pen-
itential movement underlying his own tragicomedy and romance.[28]
At the same time, Malevole's striking satiric persona and the play's
evocation of courtly decadence pointed the way for Tourneur's and
Webster's development of Italianate anti-court tragedy. It is a tribute to the breadth of Marston's artistic achievement that *The
Malcontent* could initiate two such different dramatic forms.

The Play on the Stage

1. At the Blackfriars theatre

The original version of *The Malcontent* was as carefully calculated
for performance at the Blackfriars by the Children of the Queen's
Revels as it was written for the taste of the elite, court-oriented

---

[28] See Thomas A. Pendleton, 'Shakespeare's Disguised Duke Play', in *'Fanned and
Winnowed Opinions': Shakespearean Essays Presented to Harold Jenkins*, ed.
Mahon and Pendleton (1987), and Bennett, *op. cit.*

audience that attended there. Charging six times the admission price of public theatres like the Globe or Fortune for its cheapest seats, the Blackfriars attracted a select audience with a high proportion of Inns of Court residents, fashionable gallants, gentlewomen, and lords and ladies who filled its side-boxes or displayed themselves by sitting on stools on the stage itself. In contrast to the unroofed public theatres, the light from the windows of its indoor auditorium was supplemented by candles and so gave an illusionistic effect to interior scenes and depictions of court revels or processions, which the boy companies favoured over the noisy drum-and-trumpet battles staged in the public playhouses. A special feature of its entertainment was music, for the boy actors were also skilled as vocalists and instrumentalists and, according to a German visitor of 1602, presented 'a delightful instrumental concert played on organs, lutes, pandorins, mandolins, violins, and flutes' for a whole hour before the plays began.[29] Music was also performed between the acts. The personnel of the children's companies included many young enough to fill the relatively large number of women's roles in their plays, but others would have been older boys able to play adult roles persuasively. Despite their youth, they were trained in rhetorical presentation, and so employed acting styles that ranged from self-conscious mimicry to a more serious, declamatory style.[30]

The Malcontent was clearly designed to take advantage of these features. The women's parts do not seem to have been doubled, for although Emilia does not speak in the final masque, she enters in V.v and is not directed to exit, leaving five women on stage at the play's end. In general, the actors' parts are written so that the expression of emotion would be within the boys' capacities. Thus Pietro's grief and anger at Aurelia's infidelity is expressed most fully in his account in IV.iii of his supposed suicide, a self-conscious piece of rhetoric in which emotion is both heightened and distanced by being presented as third-person narrative. Stage-combat, too, is carefully controlled, for the relatively small stage at the Blackfriars encouraged witplay, rather than swordplay.[31] Though Mendoza bares his chest to Pietro's sword in the manner of Richard III and later runs Ferneze through as he exits from Aurelia's bedchamber, there is no real duelling. When the revengers surround Mendoza in the final masque, they draw pistols rather than swords, perhaps a necessary accommodation to a playing-space that seems to have been only twenty-six feet wide at most. At the same time, the stage

[29] Translated by Irwin Smith, Shakespeare's Blackfriars Playhouse (1964), p. 551
[30] See Michael Shapiro, Children of the Revels (1977)
[31] See Andrew Gurr, 'Playing in Amphitheatres and Playing in Hall Theatres', ET, 13 (1994)

must have been deep enough for the actors to travel some distance before addressing the audience; at several points characters entering are perceived by those onstage before their entrance is formally noted in the stage directions or before they engage in conversation. Marston's stage-directions also confirm the theory that the Blackfriars stage was always lighted, either through candles or daylight from the upper windows, for they make no special mention of lights for daytime scenes, but do call for properties to signal darkness. Thus the torches and lantern used for the midnight assignation of Ferneze and Aurelia (see stage directions to II.i) seem to have been as much realistic as illusionistic, though the extra lights employed for the masque in V.v would have shone more brightly on the indoor stage than in the open-air public theatres.[32]

The main element that defines *The Malcontent* as a Blackfriars play, however, is its musical quality. Marston exploits the musical capabilities of the company by including four songs, a fully-staged masque, and additional instrumental music, often used in significant ways. So 'the vilest out-of-tune music' by which Malevole announces his presence in the first scene (which would have contrasted sharply with the melodies of the Blackfriars prelude) is emblematic of the moral disorder of Pietro's court, and the dance music on which Aurelia insists in IV.ii expresses her defiant indifference to Pietro's fate. The fifth-act masque not only captures the bustling preparation preceding court entertainments, but also figures the reordering of Genoese society as the white-robed nobles reunite with their wives and drive Mendoza out of the court, restoring right rule and harmony.[33] As first presented 'with the soul of lively action' and the musical resources of the Blackfriars company, *The Malcontent* must have been an impressive show.

2. At the Globe theatre

When the King's Men acquired Marston's play for performance at the Globe, they obtained a script that would both appeal to sophisticated tastes and also provide a suitable vehicle for the talents of their lead actor, Richard Burbage, who played the Malcontent. Already known for his performance as Hamlet, Burbage would have fitted easily into a role calling for him to taunt Pietro and Mendoza in an 'antic' manner as Hamlet taunts Polonius and Claudius. Unfortunately, we cannot know with certainty whether Marston's 'augmentations' to Altofronto-Malevole's part had been written earlier or were designed specifically for Burbage. They explain Altofronto's motives, let him stimulate Pietro's jealousy

[32] See Robert Graves, 'Elizabethan Lighting Effects', *RD*, n.s. 12 (1987)
[33] See Christian Kieffer, 'Music and Marston's *The Malcontent*', *SP*, 51 (1954)

more graphically, underscore his contempt for Bilioso's obsequious time-serving, and clarify the play's political moral. The added emphasis on Bilioso's duplicity elevates him to a major thematic role in the play. His attempt to excuse himself after Altofronto removes his disguise is reminiscent of Shakespeare's Lucio in *Measure for Measure*, another sign of Shakespeare's familiarity with, and creative imitation of, Marston's drama.

Webster's additions, in contrast to Marston's, present Bilioso less as an unprincipled flatterer than as an affected fool and braggart who plays the straight-man to his wife Bianca and the jester Passarello. A witty, 'artificial' fool like Shakespeare's Touchstone and Feste, Passarello's part was certainly written for Robert Armin, the actor who performed those roles. Webster's dialogue draws on the same repertory of comic devices employed by the clever Shakespearean clown – satirical flashes at court and city, witty similes, bawdy puns, and mock logic like his demonstration in V.i that quarrellers are the greatest cowards. Passarello's part would have provided an excellent demonstration of Armin's skills and added a lighter dimension to Marston's biting satire. Another light touch of a kind familiar to the Globe audience is the entirely gratuitous joke about whores and punks in England that seems to have been inserted at V.iv.17–30 merely for its similarity to the Gravedigger's jest in *Hamlet* about the madness of Englishmen.

The cleverest of Webster's additions, however, is the Induction. A witty piece of in-group humour, it features Will Sly, an actor in the King's Men, playing a stubborn gallant. Sly insists on sitting on a stool on the stage as he had at the Blackfriars (something not done at the Globe, where it would hinder the audience's view) and demands to talk to the leading actors, naming – among others – Will Sly! Accompanied by his foolishly naive cousin, played by the skinny John Sinklo, Sly speaks contemptuously both of the garlic-eating groundlings and the 'gentleman' auditors, in effect encouraging the audience to side with the King's Men against his obnoxious character as he complains about the inferiority of their acting and the bitterness of the play's satire. Webster thus neutralises potential objections to the King's Men's performance by building them into his Induction, a technique often used in the private theatres.[34] The Induction continues to amuse knowledgeable readers, but it no doubt had a short dramatic life, for the King's Men themselves took over the theatre at Blackfriars in 1608 when the Children of the Revels was dissolved. Marston's play was apparently retained in the repertory through the Caroline period, for John Greene mentions in his diary that he saw it performed in February 1634/5.[35]

---

[34] See Shapiro, *op. cit.*
[35] Quoted in G. E. Bentley, *The Jacobean and Caroline Stage*, I (1941), p. 123

3. Modern productions

The Malcontent was not performed during the Restoration period or the eighteenth-century, no doubt because its narrative complexity and its style of wit did not conform to the taste of the times. It was finally revived in July of 1850 by the courageous manager George Bolton, who presented it at the Olympic Theatre in London with a cast that included James Johnstone as Malevole, W. Atwood as Passarello, and Mrs. Griffiths as Maquerelle, all of whom were singled out for special notice by the reviewer for *The Weekly Dispatch* of 4 August. The critics, however, were divided about the merits of both the cast and the play. As presented by Johnstone, Malevole's railing seemed to several to be mere rant, and the play itself was judged by *The Times* (30 July) to be only 'a dramatic curiosity'. The critic for *The Observer* acknowledged that the production 'was carefully got up and respectably acted', but objected to Marston's writing, which did not sufficiently portray virtue in distress in the manner of contemporary melodrama. Admitting that Marston 'had a knowledge of human nature, was a shrewd satirist of the follies and vices of his time, and his plays are full of pregnant sayings', the reviewer nevertheless complained that 'they are also polluted by coarse and filthy ribaldry; and his serious passages indicate neither the tenderness, passion, imagination, nor splendour of poetical diction, for which the writers of that age were distinguished'.[36] His reactions testify to the cultural collision between Victorian standards of propriety and Marston's racy satire, but the audience apparently found the play less objectionable. The production had originally been intended for six performances only, yet paired on different occasions with such works as *A Roland for Oliver*, *The Spitalfields Weaver*, *Don Juan*, and Fielding's *Pasquin*, it ran for eighteen nights between 29 July and 20 August.

The Malcontent was not staged again until the mode of 'black comedy' became fashionable in the 1960s. In that decade it was given two student productions, first at the opening of the Nuffield Theatre at Southampton University on 6–7 March 1964, directed by Jocelyn Powell, and then in June 1968 by the Oxford University Dramatic Society in the garden of Wadham College, directed by Alan Strachan. Despite its outdoor setting, perhaps a little too idyllic for the satiric tone of the early scenes, Strachan's production was praised for its 'compelling dramatic and pictorial power'.[37] The masquers processed through the audience to the tune of a stately galliard, imposingly hieratic in their white robes and gilded masks, and both Aurelia's moral transformation and the Passarello-Bilioso

[36] Quoted by Michael Scott, *John Marston's Plays* (1978), p. 117
[37] *The Oxford Times*, 21 June 1968

Malevole (Derek Godfrey) and Mendoza (Michael Johnson)
from the 1973 Nottingham Playhouse production, directed by
Jonathan Miller. By courtesy of Nottingham Playhouse

passages (judiciously trimmed) came across more effectively than
expected.[38] The contrast of the clown's nonsensical matter and
Malevole's 'mordant, cutting wit' appealed to contemporary taste,
and Marston's portrayal of scheming and lustfulness was adjudged
to be still topical. Both of these productions exploited the play's
potential for spectacular display, employing sumptuous period costumes to suggest the splendour of a Renaissance court. Their
approach was rejected by Dominic Dromgoole, who mounted a
modern-dress version with rock music at the A. D. C. Theatre in
Cambridge in May 1983.

The Malcontent's one modern professional production, directed
by Jonathan Miller for the Nottingham Playhouse in April of 1973
and staged again in June in Sam Wanamaker's tent theatre at the
Globe site in London, presented it as a tragic farce. Conceiving of
the work as 'a slapstick tragedy' that 'has all the mad attack and

[38] These details are derived from a letter by Mr. Strachan to G. K. Hunter, graciously
shared with me by Prof. Hunter

insane surrealism of the Goon Show' (a zany radio programme), Miller invested the Genoese court with sombre elegance but undercut its dignity with stage business that featured 'pratfalls, unison movement, and rapid-fire delivery'.[39] The set by Patrick Robertson consisted of three dark arches decorated with shadowy statuary, and the costumes by Rosemary Vercoe were made of thick sackcloth, in tones of white, grey, and black. The decadent courtiers were presented in stylised tableaux and reduced to comic marionettes in white facial make-up, white tights, and oversized ruffs. The result, as described by the reviewer for *Stage*, was 'a stiff surrealism, with more than a touch of ashen corpses, a whiff of zombies set in motion by the malcontent himself'.[40] By contrast, Derek Godfrey as Malevole was 'real and ruddy', shattering the sonorous music of the accompanying brass consort with discordant notes from a battered alto horn. Dressed in a baggy hat and a coat that reached to his ankles, Godfrey gave an animated, versatile performance. Irving Wardle described him as 'exploding into hen-like cluckings, little dances on the balls of his feet, and nasal mimicry of court manners',[41] while Benedict Nightingale reported that 'he yaps, jumps and fawns like a lapdog, mimes a hilarious, gobbling, chucking death and yet is credibly grave and princely when he must be'.[42] Though Godfrey's spirited acting dominated the show, most reviewers felt he was effectively supported by a cast that included Arthur Cox as Pietro, Michael Johnson as Mendoza, Eve Belton as Aurelia, and Hazel Hughes as Maquerelle. Critical debate about the production centered mainly on the question of whether the slapstick overwhelmed the play's tragicomic seriousness. Gary O'Connor observed that 'Mr Miller's approach ... is to take the moral core of the play seriously – as, for instance, in Meg Davies' ferocious assertion of loyalty, as Maria, to her deposed husband',[43] and Robert Cushman affirmed that Miller 'has accurately located the play's lunatic gusto, and has, more surprisingly, done serious justice to its fits of morality'.[44] On the other hand, Nicholas de Jongh argued that 'the Jacobean[s] thought Italy corrupt, not silly' and condemned the production because 'the moral seriousness goes for nothing'.[45]

Balancing the different elements of *The Malcontent* in performance is obviously no small challenge, but one that is worth the

[39] *The Observer*, 22 April 1973
[40] *Stage*, 3 May 1973
[41] *The Times*, 12 April 1973
[42] *The New Statesman*, 20 April 1973
[43] *The Financial Times*, 14 April 1973
[44] *The Observer*, 17 June 1973
[45] *The Guardian*, 14 June 1973

Malevole (Derek Godfrey) and Duke Pietro (Arthur Cox) in
III.v. By courtesy of Nottingham Playhouse

Mendoza (Michael Johnson) confronted by the masquers in
V.vi. By courtesy of Nottingham Playhouse

effort. It takes a deft theatrical touch to do justice both to its railing satire and its comic ironies, to its grim assessment of human corruption and its hopeful vision of social and spiritual renewal. Yet like Shakespeare's problem comedies, which have attracted considerable theatrical and critical interest in recent years, the dark comedy of *The Malcontent* is once again accessible to modern audiences. One would hope to see it staged more frequently in the future.

NOTE ON THE TEXT

The printing history of *The Malcontent* is tangled, and conse-
quently the play poses some unusual challenges to an editor. Its
three quarto editions (STC 17479, 17480, 17481) were all printed
in 1604 by Valentine Simmes for William Aspley. The first, here
called Q1, contains the shortest version of the text. Part of the printing was apparently farmed out, for sheets B–E are set in a type
identified with the printing house of George Eld, while sheets F–H
were set by Simmes' Compositor A, who is identifiable by his distinctive handling of speech prefixes and has been observed to alter
his copytext every sixteen lines on average. Marston speaks apolo-
getically in his epistle 'To the Reader' of his 'enforced absence'
during the printing, and Q1, though lightly corrected in press, contains numerous errors of the type likely to result from misreading
manuscript copy. These are corrected and some revisions of an
authorial nature are made in Q2, which introduces new errors, but
adds ten lines apparently omitted from IV.v, as well as the
'Epilogus' and, in some copies, the 'Prologus'. The printing of the
second quarto (Q2) must have followed closely upon the first
edition, for sheets A, D and E of Q2 seem to have been printed from
standing type. However, sheets F–I were entirely reset, and Martin
Wine has discovered that sheets B and G of the copy in the Carl H.
Pforzheimer library were recast yet once more while in press.
Although sheets F–H of Q2 handle speech prefixes in much the
same way as they are presented in the second division of Q1, they
contain numerous variations in spelling. The third quarto (Q3) adds
the 'augmentations' by Marston and the induction and new scenes
by Webster discussed above, but in the main body of the text almost
as many errors are introduced as are corrected. Shares of the printing seem to have been reversed in this edition, so that the composi-
tor(s) who set sheets F–H of Q1–2 assumed responsibility for sheets
A–G of Q3, while sheets H and I were set by the compositor of
sheets B–E, and I in Q2 (Hunter suspects three compositors, with
the third responsible for sheets A–C). Once again there are a high
number of spelling changes in sheets A–G, while punctuation has
been systematically revised and upgraded, though sometimes mistakenly so. In a few places someone has also eliminated many of the
colloquial features of Malevole's and Maquerelle's speech, altering
'i' th'' to 'in the', 'ha'' to 'have', 'ye' to 'you' or 'thou', and 'does'
to 'doth'. These changes, however, are not made consistently:
Malevole's query at II.ii.9 is altered to 'how doth Janivere thy husband?' but followed by 'Does he hawk a-nights still?' (l. 11); his
exclamation 'Ha, ye huge rascal!' (III.iii.40) is altered to 'you', but

Bilioso's 'Hence, ye gross-jawed, peasantly –' (II.iii.30) is unchanged; and Maquerelle's question to the ladies, 'Will you sit and eat?' (see II.iv.5), is inconsistent with her usual plural, 'beauties, I would ha' ye once wise' (IV.i.27–8). Since D. J. Lake has established that Marston prefers 'ye' and 'ha'' and uses 'does' more heavily than 'doth' after 1602 (but not before), it seems doubtful that Marston is responsible for Q3's alterations.[46]

The present edition is based on a comparison of the corrected states of the three early quartos, using as its exemplars the Folger Library's Copy 1 of STC 17479, the British Museum's copy C.39.c.25 of Q2, and for Q3 the facsimile of the British Museum's Ashley 3625 as corrected by B.M. C.34.e.17 and B.M. C.12.g.8. It takes Q3 as its copy text, but follows Hunter and Jackson & Neill in rejecting the altered speech forms of Q3 on the grounds that they are inappropriate to the character of Maquerelle and the disguised Malevole. For reasons explained in the notes, I have introduced two new emendations at V.iv.91 and V.vi.71. The notes indicate substantive variants from the copy text and some alternative readings in the earlier quartos, but merely identify press corrections and pass over obvious misprints such as turned letters. Spelling, capitalisation, and punctuation have been modernised, though I have tried to exercise some tact in regards to the latter, seeking a middle ground between the fluid, unpointed series in the early texts and the heavily punctuated phrases and shorter periods of some modern editions. Marston's manuscript was apparently not lineated clearly, and the quartos sometimes shift back and forth from prose to blank verse, varied by occasional tetrameter or hexameter lines. Where the compositors seem to have mistaken verse for prose, I have followed Dyce and other editors by printing it as verse, but passages where Marston seems to have intentionally mingled the two forms have

---

[46] Wine's 1964 edition was the first based on an extensive collation of multiple copies; for a fuller listing of variants and a table of press corrections, see Hunter. Akihiro Yamada has published detailed studies of compositorial preferences and stop-press corrections in *Poetry and Drama of the English Renaissance in Honour of Professor Jiro Ozu* (Tokyo, 1980), pp. 107–32; and in *Studies in Humanities* (Shinshu University), vol. 14 (March, 1980), 121–5; vol. 17 (March, 1983), 93–113; and vol. 22, (March, 1988), 53–9. For Simmes' compositors and typefaces, see W. Craig Ferguson, *Valentine Simmes* (Charlottesville, Virginia, 1968); Alan E. Craven, 'The Reliability of Simmes's Compositor A', *SB*, 32 (1979), 186–97; and Adrian Weiss, 'Font Analysis as a Bibliographic Method: The Elizabethan Play-quarto Printers and Compositors', *SB*, 43 (1990), 95–163. For Marston's linguistic habits, see the study of Webster's additions by Lake, cited above in the Introduction, fn. 11, and for his punctuation, Anthony Graham-White *Punctuation and Its Dramatic Value in Shakespearean Drama* (Newark and London, 1995), pp. 105–17.

been left as they are. Finally, two distinctive features of his text have been retained even though they are inconsistent with modern practice. First, since Marston seems to have consciously aimed at an aphoristic style, I have used italics to indicate all passages specially marked as sententious in Q3, regardless of whether they were originally italicised or set off by inverted commas. Secondly, I have retained Marston's neo-classic scene divisions, which usually (though not always) indicate a new scene when a new character enters, rather than employing the clear-stage test used by Shakespearean editors. To use the latter method would produce disproportionate scenes, making I.i–v, for example, one long scene and seeming to mark a major break at I.vi, when the action is really continuous and imagined to take place in apartments at court, as the reentry of Mendoza later in the scene indicates. Marston's own divisions, unfortunately, sometimes obscure the major units of the action, for Malevole's public performance in the opening scenes contrasts with his private dialogue with Pietro, and his soliloquy and dialogue with Celso at the end of I.iii and the beginning of I.iv reveal him as Altofronto but are run on into his resumption of role-playing with Bilioso. Marston's divisions, however, may at least give readers and actors a rough sense of major shifts as characters come and go, and using them where possible makes references in the New Mermaid more compatible with other editions that follow Q3. I have added a scene division after V.i.53, for Webster's addition calls for a clear stage after the exit of Bilioso and Passarello, making the entry of Malevole and Maquerelle that originally began Act V a new scene.

FURTHER READING

This list does not include items already mentioned in the Introduction.

Katherine Armstrong, 'Possets, Pills and Poisons: Physicking the Female Body in Early Seventeenth-Century Drama', *Cahiers Élisabéthains*, 61(2002), 43–56

William Babula, 'The Avenger and the Satirist: John Marston's Malevole', *ET*, 6 (1978), 48–58

Anthony Caputi, *John Marston: Satirist* (1961)

Charles Cathcart, 'John Marston, *The Malcontent*, and the King's Men', *RES*, n.s. 57 (2006), 43–63

Larry S. Champion, '*The Malcontent* and the Shape of Elizabethan-Jacobean Comedy', *SEL*, 25 (1985), 361–79

Ira S. Clark, 'Character and Cosmos in Marston's *Malcontent*', *Modern Language Studies*, 13 (1983), 80–96

R. A. Foakes, 'On Marston, *The Malcontent*, and *The Revenger's Tragedy*', *ET*, 6 (1978), 59–75

Brian Gibbons, *Jacobean City Comedy*, 2nd ed. (1980)

William M. Hamlin, 'Temporizing as Pyrrhonizing in Marston's *The Malcontent*', *Comparative Drama*, 34 (2000), 305–19

Steven Hayward, '"I'll make one i' the masque": John Marston's *The Malcontent* and the Appropriation of the Masque', *Renaissance Papers 1998*, ed. T. H. Howard-Hill and Philip Rollinson, 69–79

Donald K. Hedrick, 'The Masquing Principle in Marston's *The Malcontent*', *ELR*, 8 (1978), 24–42

Ejner J. Jensen, 'Theme and Imagery in *The Malcontent*', *SEL*, 10 (1970), 367–84

Alvin Kernan, *The Cankered Muse* (1959)

R. W. Ingram, *John Marston* (1978)

Charles Osborne McDonald, *The Rhetoric of Tragedy* (1966)

Douglas F. Rutledge, 'The Politics of Disguise', in *The Witness of Times*, ed. Katherine Z. Keller and Gerald J. Schiffhorst (1993)

John Peter, *Complaint and Satire in Early English Literature* (1956)

Brownell Salomon, 'The Theological Basis of Imagery and Structure in *The Malcontent*', *SEL*, 14 (1974), 271–84

James Edward Siemon, 'Disguise in Marston and Shakespeare', *Huntington Library Quarterly*, 38 (1974–75), 106–23

Albert H. Tricomi, *Anticourt Drama in England 1603–1642* (1989)

T. F. Wharton, ed., *The Drama of John Marston: Critical Re-visions* (2000)

Opposite: Title-page of Q3, 1604, by courtesy of The British Library (British Library, Ashley 3625)

THE

MALCONTENT.

Augmented by *Marston*.

With the Additions played by the Kings
Maiesties seruants.

Written by *Ihon Webster*.

1 6 0 4.

AT LONDON
Printed by V.S. for William Aspley, and
are to be sold at his shop in Paules
Church·yard.

BENIAMINO JONSONIO
POETAE
ELEGANTISSIMO
GRAVISSIMO

AMICO
SUO CANDIDO ET CORDATO,
IOHANNES MARSTON
MUSARUM ALUMNUS

ASPERAM HANC SUAM THALIAM
D.D.

Dedication 'To his forthright and judicious friend, the most polished and weighty poet Ben Jonson, John Marston, disciple of the Muses, gives and dedicates this, his rough comedy.'
BENIAMINO Q1–2 (BENIAMINI Q3)
ASPERAM perhaps in the double sense of 'rough' or 'unpolished' and 'bitter'
THALIAM Thalia is the Muse of comedy, here used metonymically
D. D. *'Dat Dedicatque'*

3

To the Reader

I am an ill orator and, in truth, use to indite more honestly
than eloquently, for it is my custom to speak as I think and
write as I speak.

In plainness, therefore, understand that in some things I
have willingly erred, as in supposing a Duke of Genoa and in   5
taking names different from that city's families; for which
some may wittily accuse me, but my defence shall be as honest
as many reproofs unto me have been most malicious, since, I
heartily protest, it was my care to write so far from reasonable offence that even strangers in whose state I laid my scene   10
should not from thence draw any disgrace to any, dead or
living. Yet in despite of my endeavours, I understand some
have been most unadvisedly over-cunning in misinterpreting
me and with subtlety as deep as hell have maliciously spread
ill rumours, which, springing from themselves, might to them-   15
selves have heavily returned. Surely I desire to satisfy every
firm spirit who in all his actions proposeth to himself no more
ends than God and virtue do, whose intentions are always
simple; to such I protest that with my free understanding I
have not glanced at disgrace of any but of those whose   20
unquiet studies labour innovation, contempt of holy policy,
reverend comely superiority, and established unity; for the
rest of my supposed tartness, I fear not but unto every worthy
mind it will be approved so general and honest as may modestly pass with the freedom of a satire. I would fain leave the   25
paper, only one thing afflicts me – to think that scenes
invented merely to be spoken should be enforcively published
to be read and that the least hurt I can receive is to do myself

---

1 *orator* petitioner
   indite compose, write
7 *wittily* knowingly
12–15 *some … rumours* Marston is defending himself here, as he will again in the
   Prologue, against charges that his characters are satiric representations of real
   people.
14 *subtlety* Q1–2 (subtilitie Q3)
20–2 *whose … unity* whose restless efforts seek to induce revolution and to bring
   into contempt the divinely ordained political order (or 'religious policies'), the
   dignity of proper authority, and the unity of the established church
26–9 *scenes … wrong* Marston here makes the common Renaissance excuse, not
   always credible, that he is publishing his work only to forestall an unauthorised
   edition that he cannot prevent.
27 *merely* only, exclusively

the wrong. But since others otherwise would do me more, the
least inconvenience is to be accepted. I have myself, therefore,   30
set forth this comedy, but so that my enforced absence must
much rely upon the printer's discretion; but I shall intreat,
slight errors in orthography may be as slightly overpassed and
that the unhandsome shape which this trifle in reading presents may be pardoned for the pleasure it once afforded you   35
when it was presented with the soul of lively action.

Sine aliqua dementia nullus Phoebus.
J. M.

---

37 *Sine ... Phoebus* Q2–3. 'No poet is without some madness' (based on a quotation from Aristotle in Seneca, *De Tranquillitate Animi* xvii.10), replacing Q1's
motto, *Me mea sequentur fata* ('Let my destiny pursue me').

[Members of the King's Men who appear in the Induction written for the Globe Theatre

WILLIAM SLY, as a young gallant
JOHN SINKLO, as his cousin, young Doomsday
RICHARD BURBAGE
HENRY CONDELL   } as themselves
JOHN LOWIN
A TIRE-MAN]

WILLIAM SLY a founding member of the Lord Chamberlain's Men, the company
formed in 1594 which was relicensed as the King's Men in 1603. Later he was a
sharer in the ownership of the Globe and Blackfriars.

JOHN SINKLO or Sincler, a minor actor in the company, customarily given secondary
roles, and noted for his thinness. See Allison Gaw's article on him in *Anglia*,
XLIX (1926), 289–303.

RICHARD BURBAGE the leading actor in the company from the early 1590s to his death
in 1619. In addition to playing the title role in *The Malcontent*, he acted Richard
III, Hamlet, Lear, and Othello.

HENRY CONDELL Like Burbage, he was one of the managers of the King's Company.
He played the villainous Cardinal in Webster's *The Duchess of Malfi*.

JOHN LOWIN first appears in dramatic records as a member of Worcester's Men in
1602 but performed with the King's Men in Jonson's *Sejanus* sometime in 1603.
A man of great size, he played both 'honest' soldiers and villains.

TIRE-MAN property man

THE INDUCTION

Written for the Globe Theatre

Enter w. SLY, *a* TIRE-MAN *following him with a stool*
[SLY *sits at the side of the stage front*]

TIRE-MAN
　Sir, the gentlemen will be angry if you sit here.
SLY
　Why? We may sit upon the stage at the private house. Thou
　dost not take me for a country gentleman, dost? Dost think
　I fear hissing? I'll hold my life thou took'st me for one of
　the players.   5
TIRE-MAN
　No sir.
SLY
　By God's lid, if you had, I would have given you but six-
　pence for your stool. Let them that have stale suits sit in the
　galleries. Hiss at me! He that will be laughed out of a tavern
　or an ordinary shall seldom feed well or be drunk in good   10
　company. Where's Harry Condell, Dick Burbage, and Will
　Sly? Let me speak with some of them.
TIRE-MAN
　An't please you to go in, sir, you may.
SLY
　I tell you, no; I am one that hath seen this play often and

The Induction for the Globe Theatre written by John Webster and printed only in Q3;
　　see the Introduction, p. xxxi

　2 *sit ... house* The indoor Blackfriars Theatre, where self-display by the more gen-
　　　teel audience was a part of the theatrical ritual. At the Globe, spectators on the
　　　stage would obscure the sight-lines of the gallants in the galleries and the audi-
　　　ence in the yard.

　4 *hissing* Thomas Dekker's *Gull's Hornbook*, 1609, advises its readers to retain
　　　their seats on the stage 'though the Scarcrows in the yard hoot at you, hisse at
　　　you, spit at you, yea throw durt even in your teeth' (ed. Grosart, p. 250).

　7 *lid* ed. (slid Q3) eyelid
　8 *stale* out-of-fashion
　10 *ordinary* eating-house
　11–12 *Dick ... Sly* ed. (D: Burbage, and W: Sly Q3)
　13 *in* i.e. backstage, into the tiring house

9

can give them intelligence for their action. I have most of   15
the jests here in my table-book.

[*Exit* TIRE-MAN]

Enter SINKLO

SINKLO
Save you, coz!
SLY
O cousin, come, you shall sit between my legs here.
SINKLO
No indeed, cousin, the audience then will take me for a viol
da gamba and think that you play upon me.   20
SLY
Nay, rather that I work upon you, coz.
SINKLO
We stayed for you at supper last night at my cousin
Honeymoon's, the woollen-draper. After supper we drew
cuts for a score of apricots, the longest cut still to draw an
apricot. By this light, 'twas Mistress Frank Honeymoon's   25
fortune still to have the longest cut: I did measure for the
women. – What be these, coz?

Enter D. BURBAGE, H. CONDELL, J. LOWIN

SLY
The players. [*Rises, removes his hat, and bows*] God save
you!
BURBAGE
You are very welcome.   30
SLY
[*Indicating* SINKLO] I pray you, know this gentleman my
cousin, 'tis Master Doomsday's son, the usurer.

---

15 *intelligence ... action* descriptions of the original stage-business
16 *table-book* pocket notebook. Would-be wits who copied down other people's
    jests or vocabulary were often the target of satire; compare Shakespeare's Sir
    Andrew Aguecheek in *Twelfth Night* III.i.83 ff.
17 *coz* cousin, but like it, often used to mean 'friend'
19–20 *viol da gamba* ancestor of the modern cello
23–4 *drew cuts* drew lots, using straws or sticks of different lengths, possibly with
    a bawdy play on 'cut', the female genitalia
24 *still* always
32 *usurer* Appropriately named since at Doomsday, the Last Judgement, he in turn
    will be judged if he has shown no mercy to borrowers whose bonds fall due.

CONDELL
I beseech you, sir, be covered.

SLY
No, in good faith, for mine ease – look you, my hat's the
handle to this fan. [*Fans himself*] God's so, what a beast   35
was I, I did not leave my feather at home! Well, but I'll take
an order with you.   *Puts his feather in his pocket*

BURBAGE
Why do you conceal your feather, sir?

SLY
Why? Do you think I'll have jests broken upon me in the
play, to be laughed at? This play hath beaten all your gal-   40
lants out of the feathers: Blackfriars hath almost spoiled
Blackfriars for feathers.

SINKLO
God's so, I thought 'twas for somewhat our gentlewomen
at home counselled me to wear my feather to the play, yet
I am loath to spoil it.   45

SLY
Why, coz?

SINKLO
Because I got it in the tiltyard. There was a herald broke my
pate for taking it up, but I have worn it up and down the
Strand and met him forty times since, and yet he dares not
challenge it.   50

SLY
Do you hear, sir, this play is a bitter play.

33 *be covered* Elizabethan gallants normally wore hats. Sly has removed his as a sign
   of respect; his refusal to put it on again echoes Osric's language in *Hamlet*
   V.ii.105.
35 *fan* the conspicuously large feather in his hat, another sign of affected gallantry
36 *feather* ed. (father Q3)
40–2 *This play ... feathers* See the jest about fools and feathers at V.iii.39. Sly
   implies that Marston's satire has affected the feather trade, also located in the
   Blackfriars area near the playhouse.
43 *God's so* a milder version of 'Catso' (from It. *cazzo* = penis)
47 *tiltyard* Sinklo's plume has come cheap, having fallen off someone's helmet
   during a jousting at Whitehall, refereed by heralds with batons. His story is reminiscent of the would-be gallant Stephen's parading in Downright's mislaid cloak
   in Jonson's *Every Man in His Humour* IV.vii and xi.
49 *Strand* the site of fashionable shops and dwellings in London's emerging West
   End

CONDELL

Why, sir, 'tis neither satire nor moral, but the mean passage
of a history. Yet there are a sort of discontented creatures
that bear a stingless envy to great ones, and these will wrest
the doings of any man to their base malicious applyment;   55
but should their interpretation come to the test, like your
marmoset they presently turn their teeth to their tail and eat
it.

SLY

I will not go so far with you, but I say, any man that hath
wit may censure (if he sit in the twelve-penny room), and I   60
say again, the play is bitter.

BURBAGE

Sir, you are like a patron that presenting a poor scholar to
a benefice enjoins him not to rail against anything that
stands within compass of his patron's folly. Why should
not we enjoy the ancient freedom of poesy? Shall we protest   65
to the ladies that their painting makes them angels, or to
my young gallant that his expense in the brothel shall gain
him reputation? No sir, such vices as stand not accountable
to law should be cured as men heal tetters, by casting ink
upon them. Would you be satisfied in anything else, sir?   70

SLY

Ay, marry, would I. I would know how you came by this
play.

CONDELL

Faith, sir, the book was lost, and because 'twas pity so good
a play should be lost, we found it and play it.

SLY

I wonder you would play it, another company having   75
interest in it.

---

52 *moral* morality play
    mean passage insignificant episode
53–5 *a sort ... applyment* i.e. malcontents who express their own hostility to the
    nobility by misinterpreting the writings of others as personal satire
56–8 *should ... it* i.e. when challenged they eat their words, as monkeys (according
    to the naturalist Conrad Gesner, *Historia Animalium*, 1554) eat their own tails
60 *twelve-penny room* an expensive box close to the Globe stage
62–4 *Sir ... folly* Burbage compares Sly to patrons who expect the preachers they
    appoint to avoid sermonising against their vices.
66 *painting* make-up
69 *tetters* skin eruptions
71–83 See the Introduction, pp. xiv–vi

CONDELL
Why not Malevole in folio with us, as Jeronimo in decimo-
sexto with them? They taught us a name for our play: we
call it, *One for Another*.

SLY
What are your additions?   80

BURBAGE
Sooth, not greatly needful; only as your salad to your great
feast, to entertain a little more time and to abridge the not-
received custom of music in our theatre. I must leave you,
sir.   *Exit*

SINKLO
Doth he play the Malcontent?   85

CONDELL
Yes, sir.

SINKLO
I durst lay four of mine ears, the play is not so well acted as
it hath been.

CONDELL
Oh no, sir, nothing *ad Parmenonis suem*.

LOWIN
Have you lost your ears, sir, that you are so prodigal of   90
laying them?

SINKLO
Why did you ask that, friend?

LOWIN
Marry, sir, because I have heard of a fellow would offer to
lay a hundred pound wager, that was not worth five bawbees; and in this kind you might venture four of your   95
elbows. Yet God defend your coat should have so many!

SINKLO
Nay, truly, I am no great censurer, and yet I might have

77–8 *folio ... decimo-sexto* i.e. with large and small-sized actors. A folio book was
  made by folding sheets of paper once into two large leaves; a decimo-sexto by
  folding the paper four times into sixteen small leaves.

89 *ad Parmenonis suem* 'compared to Parmeno's pig'. Condell implies that Sinklo
  is like the admirers of Parmeno (see Plutarch, *Symposium* V.i), who preferred his
  imitation of a pig grunting to the real thing (in this case the superior acting of
  the adult companies).

94–5 *bawbees* Scottish coins worth an English halfpenny. Webster is probably
  satirising the poor Scots followers of King James.

95–6 *four of your elbows* Coats with four elbows were worn as a comic costume by
  fools, but given Lowin's previous allusion to poverty, he may be thinking of the
  proverbial expression 'out at elbow', meaning 'worn out'.

96 *defend* forbid

been one of the college of critics once. My cousin here hath
an excellent memory indeed, sir.

SLY

Who, I? I'll tell you a strange thing of myself, and I can tell   100
you, for one that never studied the art of memory 'tis very
strange, too.

CONDELL

What's that, sir?

SLY

Why, I'll lay a hundred pound, I'll walk but once down by
the Goldsmiths' Row in Cheap, take notice of the signs, and   105
tell you them with a breath instantly.

LOWIN

'Tis very strange.

SLY

They begin as the world did, with Adam and Eve. There's
in all just five and fifty. I do use to meditate much when I
come to plays, too. What do you think might come into a   110
man's head now, seeing all this company?

CONDELL

I know not, sir.

SLY

I have an excellent thought: if some fifty of the Grecians
that were crammed in the horse-belly had eaten garlic, do
you not think the Trojans might have smelt out their knav-   115
ery?

CONDELL

Very likely.

SLY

By God, I would they had, for I love Hector horribly.

SINKLO

Oh, but coz, coz:
'Great Alexander when he came to the tomb of Achilles   120
Spake with a big loud voice, "Oh thou thrice-blessed and
    happy!" '

---

101 *art of memory* Contemporary writers on memory urged the use of physical
    locales as mnemonic devices. See Frances Yates, *The Art of Memory* (1966).

105 *signs* shop-signs, usually pictorial

111 *this company* the audience in the Globe yard, sometimes referred to as
    'stinkards' because of their bad breath

118 *they* ed. (he Q3)

120–1 *'Great ... happy'* A mangled version of John Harvey's hexameter translation
    of Petrarch's Sonnet CLIII, printed in Gabriel Harvey's *Three proper, and wittie,
    familiar Letters* (1580).

SLY

Alexander was an ass to speak so well of a filthy cullion!

LOWIN

Good sir, will you leave the stage? I'll help you to a private room.

SLY

[*To* SINKLO] Come coz, let's take some tobacco. [*To*   125
LOWIN] Have you never a prologue?

LOWIN

Not any, sir.

SLY

Let me see, I will make one extempore: come to them, and fencing of a congee with arms and legs, be round with them – 'Gentlemen, I could wish for the women's sakes you had   130 all soft cushions; and gentlewomen, I could wish that for the men's sakes you had all more easy standings'. What would they wish more but the play now? And that they shall have instantly.

[*Exeunt*]

---

122 *cullion* a base fellow

123-4 *private room* a box

125 *tobacco* Dekker's gull is advised to be 'curious in his Tobacco' (p. 229), and Jonson's *Every Man Out of His Humour* alludes to gallants who take tobacco 'over the stage, i' the lords' room' (II.iii.172-3).

129 *fencing of a congee* making an exaggerated bow

130-2 *women's sakes ... men's sakes* Compare ll. 12-17 of the Epilogue to *As You Like It*.

131-2 *cushions ... standings* with bawdy quibbles on both terms

Note on the names (definitions in quotations are from John Florio's *A Worlde of Wordes*, 1598):

ALTOFRONTO 'high forehead' (signifying wisdom or firmness in Porta's *De Humana Physiognoma*)

MALEVOLE It. *malivolo*, 'dogged, currish, bearing ill will'

MENDOZA It. *mendoso*, 'faulty'

CELSO 'high, noble, or bright'

BILIOSO choleric, angry

PREPASSO one who walks before

FERRARDO usually linked to It. *ferrare*, 'to tag points', but this means to make metal ends for laces and so does not seem applicable

EQUATO equable

GUERRINO a warrior

PASSARELLO Q3, not in Q1–2; 'a flounder' or 'dried fish called Poor John'

BIANCA 'pretty and white, also a fish called ... a minnow'

MAQUERELLE a mackerel, a bawd or a procuress

DRAMATIS PERSONAE

GIOVANNI ALTOFRONTO, disguised [as] MALEVOLE, sometime Duke
    of Genoa
PIETRO JACOMO, Duke of Genoa
MENDOZA, a minion to the Duchess of Pietro Jacomo
CELSO, a friend to Altofront
BILIOSO, an old choleric marshal
PREPASSO, a gentleman-usher
FERNEZE, a young courtier, and enamoured on the Duchess
    [Aurelia]
FERRARDO, a minion to Duke Pietro Jacomo
EQUATO }
GUERRINO } two courtiers
PASSARELLO, fool to Bilioso

AURELIA, Duchess to Duke Pietro Jacomo
MARIA, Duchess to Duke Altofront
EMILIA }
BIANCA } two ladies attending the Duchess [Aurelia]
MAQUERELLE, an old panderess

[CAPTAIN OF THE CITADEL
MERCURY, Presenter of the masque
ATTENDANT, SUITORS, PAGES, GUARDS

Scene: Genoa]

PROLOGUE

Written for the Blackfriars Theatre

An imperfect ode, being but one staff,
spoken by the Prologue

To wrest each hurtless thought to private sense
Is the foul use of ill-bred Impudence;
Immodest censure now grows wild,   5
All over-running.
Let Innocence be ne'er so chaste,
Yet at the last
She is defiled
With too nice-brainèd cunning.   10
Oh you of fairer soul,
Control
With an Herculean arm
This harm,
And once teach all old freedom of a pen,   15
Which still must write of fools, whiles't writes of men.

PROLOGUE ed. (not in Q1, Prologus Q2–3, printed at the end of the text with italics reversed). The Induction indicates it was not used at the Globe.

1 *staff* stanza

3 i.e. to twist harmless thoughts into personal applications

10 *nice-brainèd cunning* subtle ingenuity

15 *all … pen* the licence once allowed to satiric writing

phrase is taken from Juvenal II.63, where Laronia complains that women are
held to strict standards of behaviour while effeminate males escape criticism.
Marston seems to be insisting that his satire is less blameworthy than the contemporary vice that occasions it.

THE MALCONTENT

Vexat censura columbas

Act I, Scene i

The vilest out-of-tune music being heard [above],
enter BILIOSO *and* PREPASSO

BILIOSO [*Calling to the upper stage*]
Why, how now! Are ye mad, or drunk, or both, or what?
PREPASSO
Are ye building Babylon there?
BILIOSO
Here's a noise in court! You think you are in a tavern, do
you not?
PREPASSO
You think you are in a brothel-house, do you not? – This   5
room is ill-scented.

Enter one with a perfume

So, perfume, perfume; some upon me, I pray thee. The
Duke is upon instant entrance; so, make place there.

[Act I,] Scene ii

Enter the Duke PIETRO, FERRARDO, *Count* EQUATO,
Count CELSO *before, and* GUERRINO

PIETRO
Where breathes that music?
BILIOSO
The discord, rather than the music, is heard from the mal-
content Malevole's chamber.
FERRARDO
Malevole!

Act I, Scene i ed. (Actus Primus. Sce[na] Prima. Q1–3). Throughout the text I have
   translated Marston's Latin terms for modern readers; in the original editions
   they indicated that he wished his 'Tragicomedia' to be taken as serious literature.

  2 *Babylon* the Tower of Babel, noted for the discordant language of its builders.
   For the significance of Malevole's out-of-tune music, see the Introduction, p.
   xxx.

21

MALEVOLE (*Out of his chamber*)

Yaugh! God o' man, what dost thou there? Duke's   5
Ganymede, Juno's jealous of thy long stockings. Shadow of
a woman, what wouldst, weasel? Thou lamb o' court, what
dost thou bleat for? Ah, you smooth-chinned catamite!

PIETRO

Come down, thou ragged cur, and snarl here. I give thy
dogged sullenness free liberty; trot about and bespurtle   10
whom thou pleasest.

MALEVOLE

I'll come among you, you goatish-blooded toderers, as gum
into taffeta, to fret, to fret; I'll fall like a sponge into water
to suck up, to suck up. Howl again. I'll go to church and
come to you.   [*Exit above*]   15

PIETRO

This Malevole is one of the most prodigious affections that
ever conversed with nature: a man, or rather a monster,
more discontent than Lucifer when he was thrust out of the
presence; his appetite is unsatiable as the grave, as far from
any content as from heaven. His highest delight is to pro-   20
cure others' vexation, and therein he thinks he truly serves
Heaven, for 'tis his position, whosoever in this earth can be
contented is a slave and damned; therefore does he afflict all
in that to which they are most affected. The elements strug-

---

6 *Ganymede* Jove's boyish cup-bearer and favourite, resented by his wife Juno
   long stockings metonymy for 'handsome legs'; Ferrardo is wearing short trunk
   hose that display them fully. See M. Channing Linthicum, *Costume in the
   Drama of Shakespeare and his Contemporaries* (Oxford, 1936), pp. 204–6 and
   Plate X.

8 *catamite* boy kept for sexual purposes

9 *ragged* Q3 (rugged Q1–2) shaggy

10 *dogged sullenness* like that of the Cynic (Grk. *kunikos* = dog-like) philosophers,
   noted for their caustic wit and contempt of pleasure
   bespurtle urinate on (continuing the canine metaphor)

12 *goatish-blooded* lustful
   toderers an obscure term, possibly meaning 'old lechers'

12–13 *gum ... fret* gum was used as a stiffener in fabric, but made it chafe (fret)

14 *go to church* Q2–3 (pray Q1)

16 *prodigious affections* monstrous dispositions

19 *presence* presence chamber, where the monarch holds audience. Pietro imagines
   heaven as a Renaissance court.

23 *slave* i.e. contemptibly servile

24 *affected* inclined

24–5 i.e. Malevole lacks the harmonious balance of hot, cold, moist and dry attri-
   butes characteristic of a well-ordered being whose reason controls his emotions

gle within him; his own soul is at variance within herself;   25
his speech is halter-worthy at all hours. I like him, faith; he
gives good intelligence to my spirit, makes me understand
those weaknesses which others' flattery palliates. – Hark!
They sing.

A song

[Act I,] Scene iii

Enter MALEVOLE *after the song*

PIETRO
See, he comes. Now shall you hear the extremity of a mal-
content: he is as free as air; he blows over every man. – And
sir, whence come you now?
MALEVOLE
From the public place of much dissimulation, the church.
PIETRO
What did'st there?   5
MALEVOLE
Talk with a usurer; take up at interest.
PIETRO
I wonder what religion thou art of?
MALEVOLE
Of a soldier's religion.
PIETRO
And what dost thou think makes most infidels now?

25 *within herself* Q3 (not in Q1–2)
26 *halter-worthy ... hours* good reason to hang him at any time
29 s.d. *A song* ed. (not in Q3; Q1–2, placed after Scena Tertia)

2 *free ... man* Compare Shakespeare's *As You Like It* II.vii.47–9, where Jaques
   insists on 'liberty ... / To blow on whom I please'.
4 *the church* Q1, Q3 (not in Q2). In some copies of Q1 and 3 it has been cut or
   blacked out, presumably on the censor's orders. The references to 'dissimulation'
   here and to usurers in l. 6 seem to imply that churchmen are ethically corrupt or
   hypocritical.
6 *take up* borrow
7 *art of?* Q3 (art? Q1–2)
8 *a soldier's religion* like that of the Swiss mercenary mentioned below at
   I.viii.47–8, who will 'be of any side for most money'
9 *thou* Q1–2 (not in Q3) probably, as in l. 11 below, a compositorial omission.
   See the 'Note on the Text' above, pp. xxxvii–ix.

MALEVOLE

Sects, sects. I have seen seeming Piety change her robe so　10
oft, that sure none but some arch-devil can shape her a new
petticoat.

PIETRO

Oh, a religious policy.

MALEVOLE

But damnation on a politic religion! I am weary; would I
were one of the Duke's hounds now.　　　　　　　　　15

PIETRO

But what's the common news abroad, Malevole? Thou
dogg'st rumour still.

MALEVOLE

Common news? Why, common words are, 'God save ye',
'Fare ye well'; common actions, flattery and cosenage;
common things, women and cuckolds. – And how does my　20
little Ferrard? Ah, ye lecherous animal! My little ferret, he
goes sucking up and down the palace into every hen's nest
like a weasel. And to what dost thou addict thy time to
now, more than to those antique painted drabs that are still
affected of young courtiers, Flattery, Pride, and Venery?　25

FERRARDO

I study languages: who dost think to be the best linguist of
our age?

MALEVOLE

Phew! The Devil. Let him possess thee, he'll teach thee to
speak all languages most readily and strangely; and great
reason, marry, he's travelled greatly i' the world and is　30
everywhere.

---

10 *Sects* Marston is satirising the variety of doctrine among Puritan extremists.

11 *new* Q1–2 (not in Q3)

13 *policy* expediency, but Malevole's reply condemns it as Machiavellian deception

14–15 *I am ... now* Q2–3 (not in Q1)

17 *dogg'st* to scent out or follow closely, continuing the Cynic imagery begun in I.ii.

19 *cosenage* cheating

20 *common* (i) shared by all (ii) frequent

22 *hen's nest* woman's bed

24 *antique painted drabs* old whores

25 *Venery* Lechery

26 *who ... best linguist?* A question also asked by the courtly pest in Donne's Satire
IV, 52–3.

28–9 *Let him ... strangely* Spirit possession was thought to bring the gift of
tongues. Compare Fitzdotterel's behaviour in Jonson's *The Devil Is an Ass* V.v.

30 *i' the* Q1–2 (in the Q3). I follow Q1–2's colloquial rhythm here as preferable to

FERRARDO

Save i' the court.

MALEVOLE

Ay, save i' the court. (*To* BILIOSO) And how does my old
muckhill overspread with fresh snow? Thou half a man,
half a goat, all a beast! How does thy young wife, old   35
huddle?

BILIOSO

Out, you improvident rascal! [*Kicking him*]

MALEVOLE

Do, kick, thou hugely-horned old Duke's ox, good Master
Make-please!

PIETRO

How dost thou live nowadays, Malevole?   40

MALEVOLE

Why, like the knight Sir Patrick Penlolians, with killing o'
spiders for my lady's monkey.

PIETRO

How dost spend the night? I hear thou never sleep'st.

MALEVOLE

Oh no, but dream the most fantastical. Oh heaven! Oh fubbery, fubbery!   45

PIETRO

Dream? What dream'st?

MALEVOLE

Why, methinks I see that signior pawn his foot-cloth, that

Q3's formal language, which is of doubtful authority. See the 'Note on the Text'
above, pp. xxxvii–viii, and l. 33 below.

33-4 *And . . . snow* Compare *The Scourge of Villainie*, VII, 154; snow = white hair.

34-5 *Thou . . . beast!* From Guarini's *Il Pastor Fido* (1602), II.vi, sig. G, where it is
applied to the rude satyr who courts Corisca. Malevole's railing at Ferrardo and
Bilioso is reminiscent of Thersites' abuse of Patroclus and Ajax in Shakespeare's
Troilus and Cressida.

36 *huddle* miser

38 *hugely-horned* i.e. often-cuckolded

39 *Make-please* (make-pleece, Qq). Hunter notes the parallel with Robert Wilson's
Sir Peter Pleaseman in *Three Ladies of London* (1584).

41 *Sir Patrick Penlolians* unidentified, but possibly intended to ridicule the Irish;
'the Irish lord, Sir Patrick' is mentioned in *The Dutch Courtesan* II.ii

42 *for* i.e. as food for. Marston is satirising trivial forms of romantic 'service'.

44-5 *fubbery* false pretence, deception

47 *foot-cloth* ornate trappings for a horse

metreza her plate; this madam takes physic that t'other
monsieur may minister to her; here is a pander jewelled;
there is a fellow in shift of satin this day that could not shift   50
a shirt t'other night; here a Paris supports that Helen;
there's a Lady Guinevere bears up that Sir Lancelot –
dreams, dreams, visions, fantasies, chimeras, imaginations,
tricks, conceits! (*To* PREPASSO) Sir Tristram Trimtram,
come aloft, jackanapes, with a whim-wham! Here's a   55
knight of the land of Catito shall play at trap with any page
in Europe, do the sword-dance with any morris-dancer in
Christendom, ride at the ring till the fin of his eyes look as
blue as the welkin, and run the wild-goose chase even with
Pompey the Huge.   60

PIETRO
You run.

MALEVOLE
To the Devil! – Now, Signor Guerrino, that thou from a
most pitied prisoner should'st grow a most loathed flatterer! – Alas, poor Celso, thy star's oppressed; thou art an
honest lord; 'tis pity.   65

EQUATO
Is't pity?

MALEVOLE
Ay, marry is't, philosophical Equato, and 'tis pity that thou

---

48 *metreza* mistress (a pseudo-Italianate form). Like 'signior' it here implies titled
status undermined by need.

48–9 *this madam ... her* For similar satire on women who pretend indisposition as
a cover for sexual intrigue, see Jonson's *Epicoene* V.ii.

50 *there is* Q3 (there Q1–2)
in shift of satin able to change from one satin suit to another

51–2 *Paris ... Lady Guinevere* types of men and women (adulterous wives? prostitutes?) who maintain lovers. Compare Morose's wish in *Epicoene* II.v to see Sir
Dauphine so poor that he needs to be supported by a prostitute.

52 *there's* Q1–2 (here's Q3). The early texts maintain a neater parallellism.

54–5 *Sir Tristram ... whim-wham* imitating the call of a monkey's trainer for him
to perform; a 'trim-tram' is a showy trifle or bit of nonsense

56 *knight of ... Catito* a youth from play-land (Spencer); the allusion is to the games
of 'cat' and 'trap', played with bats and balls or sticks

58 *ride at the ring* a sport in which a rider attempted to spear a suspended ring
fin lid

59 *welkin* sky
wild-goose chase a horse race in which the riders must follow the course of the
leader at a fixed interval

62 *Guerrino* ed. (Guerchino Qq)

64 *oppressed* in decline

being so excellent a scholar by art, should'st be so ridiculous a fool by nature. I have a thing to tell you, Duke; bid
'em avaunt, bid 'em avaunt.   70

PIETRO
  Leave us, leave us.

              Exeunt all save PIETRO *and* MALEVOLE

  Now sir, what is't?
MALEVOLE
  Duke, thou art a *becco*, a *cornuto*.
PIETRO
  How!
MALEVOLE
  Thou art a cuckold.   75
PIETRO
  Speak: unshale him quick.
MALEVOLE
  With most tumbler-like nimbleness.
PIETRO
  Who? By whom? I burst with desire!
MALEVOLE
  Mendoza is the man makes thee a horned beast; Duke, 'tis
  Mendoza cornutes thee.   80
PIETRO
  What conformance? Relate: short, short.
MALEVOLE
  As a lawyer's beard.
      There is an old crone in the court,
      Her name is Maquerelle;
      She is my mistress, sooth to say,   85
      And she doth ever tell me.
  Blurt o' rhyme, blurt o' rhyme! Maquerelle is a cunning
  bawd, I am an honest villain, thy wife is a close drab, and
  thou art a notorious cuckold. Farewell, Duke.

---

70 *avaunt* go away
73 *becco, cornuto* cuckold, horned one
76 *unshale* unshell, reveal. Compare *The Revenger's Tragedy* (ed. Gibbons)
   I.i.68–9: 'he began / By policy to open and unhusk me'.
77 *tumbler* acrobat
81 *conformance* confirmation, evidence
83–6 ed. (There ... Maquerelle/She ... me/ Q)
83 *crone* withered old woman
87 *Blurt o' rhyme* I spit on rhyming – an ironic comment on his own jingle before
   he resorts to plain speech
88 *close drab* secret whore

PIETRO

Stay, stay.   90

MALEVOLE

Dull, dull Duke, can lazy patience make lame revenge? Oh
God, for a woman to make a man that which God never
created, never made!

PIETRO

What did God never make?

MALEVOLE

A cuckold. To be made a thing that's hoodwinked with   95
kindness, whilst every rascal fillips his brows; to have a
coxcomb with egregious horns pinned to a lord's back,
every page sporting himself with delightful laughter, whilst
he must be the last must know it – pistols and poniards,
pistols and poniards!   100

PIETRO

Death and damnation!

MALEVOLE

Lightning and thunder!

PIETRO

Vengeance and torture!

MALEVOLE

Catso!

PIETRO

Oh revenge!   105

MALEVOLE

Nay, to select among ten thousand fairs
A lady far inferior to the most
In fair proportion both of limb and soul;
To take her from austerer check of parents,
To make her his by most devoutful rites,   110
Make her commandress of a better essence
Than is the gorgeous world, even of a man;
To hug her with as raised an appetite

95–9 *To be made ... know it* Hunter notes the parallel with the game of blind man's
    buff in *Il Pastor Fido* III.ii, sig. G3v–G4, here adapted by Marston as an image
    of the laughter directed at cuckolds behind their back

96 *fillips* taps sharply, implying that the cuckold is 'hit' by other people's ridicule,
    as the blindfolded victim is hit in the game

97 *coxcomb* the customary fool's cap

104 *Catso* A 'man's privy member' (Florio), used as an expletive

106–47 Addition 1 to Q3, probably by Marston. See Introduction, p. xvi.

109 *austerer check* more severe control

111 *essence* substance, entity

As usurers do their delved-up treasury
(Thinking none tells it but his private self);   115
To meet her spirit in a nimble kiss,
Distilling panting ardour to her heart;
True to her sheets, nay, diets strong his blood,
To give her height of hymeneal sweets –

PIETRO
Oh God!   120

MALEVOLE
Whilst she lisps and gives him some court *quelquechose*,
Made only to provoke, not satiate;
And yet even then the thaw of her delight
Flows from lewd heat of apprehension,
Only from strange imagination's rankness,   125
That forms the adulterer's presence in her soul
And makes her think she clips the foul knave's loins.

PIETRO
Affliction to my blood's root!

MALEVOLE
Nay, think, but think what may proceed of this:
Adultery is often the mother of incest.   130

PIETRO
Incest?

MALEVOLE
Yes, incest. Mark: Mendoza of his wife begets perchance a
daughter; Mendoza dies; his son marries this daughter. Say
you? Nay, 'tis frequent, not only probable, but no question
often acted, whilst ignorance, fearless ignorance, clasps his   135
own seed.

PIETRO
Hideous imagination!

MALEVOLE
Adultery? Why, next to the sin of simony, 'tis the most
horrid transgression under the cope of salvation.

---

114 *delved-up* dug-up, and thus joyously recovered
115 *tells* counts
118–19 *diets ... sweets* sharply curbs his own desire for other women to give her the
    greatest marital pleasure
121 *quelquechose* dainty trifle, i.e. sweet-nothing
123 *thaw of her delight* change in her frigid behaviour
124 *apprehension* anticipation, here of future pleasure with her lover
127 *clips* embraces. In Marston's *The Insatiate Countess*, II.i.256–8, Isabella simi-
    larly imagines embracing her lover, rather than the bridegroom she loathes.
136 *seed* relative
138 *simony* the sale of church office
139 *cope of salvation* the heavens

PIETRO
  Next to simony?   140
MALEVOLE
  Ay, next to simony, in which our men in next age shall not
  sin.
PIETRO
  Not sin! Why?
MALEVOLE
  Because (thanks to some churchmen) our age will leave
  them nothing to sin with. But adultery – oh dullness! –   145
  should have exemplary punishment, that intemperate
  bloods may freeze but to think it. I would damn him and all
  his generation; my own hands should do it – ha, I would
  not trust Heaven with my vengeance anything.
PIETRO
  Anything, anything, Malevole! Thou shalt see instantly   150
  what temper my spirit holds. Farewell; remember I forget
  thee not; farewell.   *Exit*
MALEVOLE
  Farewell.
  Lean thoughtfulness, a sallow meditation,
  Suck thy veins dry, distemperance rob thy sleep!   155
  The heart's disquiet is revenge most deep.
  He that gets blood, the life of flesh but spills,
  But he that breaks heart's peace, the dear soul kills.
  Well, this disguise doth yet afford me that
  Which kings do seldom hear or great men use –   160
  Free speech; and though my state's usurped,
  Yet this affected strain gives me a tongue
  As fetterless as is an emperor's.
  I may speak foolishly, ay, knavishly,
  Always carelessly, yet no one thinks it fashion   165

---

146 *should have* ed. (shue, should Q3). I follow Jackson and Neill in suspecting that
     the compositor reversed two words while misreading the ms. 'haue'. Some edi-
     tors read 'should show'.
148 *generation* offspring
149 *anything* at all
153–70 Addition 2 to Q3, probably by Marston.
154 *sallow* sickly yellow, here a sign of choler or jealousy
155 *distemperance* an imbalance of humours, mental disturbance
156–8 For the idea that a tormented life is a worse revenge than death, see Seneca,
     Medea, ll. 19–25.

To poise my breath, *for he that laughs and strikes*
Is lightly felt, or seldom struck again.
Duke, I'll torment thee; now my just revenge
From thee than crown a richer gem shall part:
Beneath God, naught's so dear as a calm heart.   ✓   170

[Act I,] Scene iv

Enter CELSO

CELSO
    My honoured lord –
MALEVOLE
    Peace, speak low – peace! Oh Celso, constant lord,
    Thou to whose faith I only rest discovered,
    Thou, one of full ten millions of men,
    That lovest virtue only for itself,   5
    Thou in whose hands old Ops may put her soul,
    Behold forever-banished Altofront,
    This Genoa's last-year's Duke. Oh truly noble,
    I wanted those old instruments of state,
    Dissemblance and suspect: I could not time it, Celso;   10
    My throne stood like a point midst of a circle,
    To all of equal nearness, bore with none;
    Reigned all alike, so slept in fearless virtue,

166 *poise my breath* weigh my words
166–7 *he . . . again* From Cornwallis, 'Of Ambition', *Essayes* (ed. Allen) p. 35, where
    Cornwallis affirms the underlying seriousness of his conversational style.
    Malevole's boast of a 'fetterless' tongue may also owe something to Cornwallis'
    remark that flattering courtiers 'guild over their fetters with the name of Pollicy'.
169 i.e. shall take from you something more valuable than your dukedom

  4 *one of* i.e. the only one in
  6 *Ops* goddess of wealth, who could trust in Celso's integrity
  9 *wanted* lacked
 10 *suspect* suspicion
    time it suit my behaviour to the times
 11 *midst of a circle* Q1 (in midst of a circle Q2; in middest of a circle Q3). A vexing
    line, which may have been either progressively corrupted or corrected into an
    iambic hexameter. I follow Q1's reading as the most metrical, but compare
    Marston's use of 'in midst' at IV.i.35.
    midst of in the middle of (see *OED*, B2)
 12 *bore with* favoured
 13 *fearless* unfearing

Suspectless, too suspectless, till the crowd
(Still lickerous of untried novelties),   15
Impatient with severer government,
Made strong with Florence, banished Altofront.
CELSO
Strong with Florence! Ay, thence your mischief rose;
For when the daughter of the Florentine
Was matched once with this Pietro, now Duke,   20
No stratagem of state untried was left,
Till you of all –
MALEVOLE   Of all was quite bereft.
Alas, Maria too, close prisonèd,
My true-faithed Duchess, i' the citadel.
CELSO
I'll still adhere; let's mutiny and die.   25
MALEVOLE
Oh no, climb not a falling tower, Celso;
'Tis well held desperation, no zeal,
Hopeless to strive with fate. Peace, temporise.
Hope, hope, that never forsak'st the wretched'st man,
Yet bidd'st me live and lurk in this disguise.   30
What? Play I well the free-breathed discontent?
Why man, we are all philosophical monarchs
Or natural fools. Celso, the court's afire;
The Duchess' sheets will smoke for't ere it be long.
Impure Mendoza, that sharp-nosed lord, that made   35
The cursèd match linked Genoa with Florence,
Now broad-horns the Duke, which he now knows.
Discord to malcontents is very manna;
When the ranks are burst, then scuffle Altofront.
CELSO
Ay, but durst –   40
MALEVOLE
'Tis gone, 'tis swallowed like a mineral;

15 *lickerous of* eager for
16 *with* of
17 *Made strong with* Supported by
20 *this* Q1–2 (his Q3)
27–8 Compare Cornwallis 'Of Friendship and Factions': 'headlong to run into mis-
    chief is not zeal but desperation' (p. 24)
28 *temporise* wait for a favourable moment. See the Introduction, pp. xxi–iv.
32–43 ed. (prose in Qq)
38 *very manna* true food from heaven
39 *scuffle Altofront* i.e. let Altofront scuffle
41 *mineral* medicine

Some way 'twill work. Phewt! I'll not shrink;
He's resolute who can no lower sink.

BILIOSO *entering,* MALEVOLE *shifteth his speech*

MALEVOLE
Oh the father of maypoles! Did you never see a fellow
whose strength consisted in his breath, respect in his office,   45
religion in his lord, and love in himself? Why then, behold.
BILIOSO
Signior –
MALEVOLE
My right worshipful lord, your court nightcap makes you
have a passing high forehead.
BILIOSO
I can tell you strange news, but I am sure you know them   50
already: the Duke speaks much good of you.
MALEVOLE
Go to, then; and shall you and I now enter into a strict
friendship?
BILIOSO
Second one another?
MALEVOLE
Yes.   55
BILIOSO
Do one another good offices?
MALEVOLE
Just. What though I called thee old ox, egregious wittol,
broken-bellied coward, rotten mummy? Yet since I am in
favour –
BILIOSO
Words of course, terms of disport. His grace presents you   60
by me a chain, as his grateful remembrance for – I am

---

43 s.d.–87 s.d. Addition 3 to Q3, probably by Marston.
43 s.d. *shifteth his speech* Malevole changes from the verse used by Altofronto into
    the colloquial prose of his alter ego, perhaps changing his accent as well.
44 *father of maypoles* The actor playing Bilioso must be tall and thin.
46 *in his lord* ed. (on his lord Q3)
48–9 *your ... forehead* i.e. Bilioso's cuckoldry results from his service at court
57 *wittol* unprotesting cuckold
60 *words of course* conventionally-used formulas
    disport merriment
61 *chain* i.e. a gold chain, fulfilling Pietro's promise at I.iii.150–1 to reward him

ignorant for what; marry, ye may impart. Yet howsoever –
come – dear friend. Dost know my son?

MALEVOLE
Your son?

BILIOSO
He shall eat woodcocks, dance jigs, make possets, and play   65
at shuttle-cock with any young lord about the court. He has
as sweet a lady, too – dost know her little bitch?

MALEVOLE
'Tis a dog, man!

BILIOSO
Believe me, a she-bitch! Oh, 'tis a good creature; thou shalt
be her servant. I'll make thee acquainted with my young   70
wife, too – what, I keep her not at court for nothing! 'Tis
grown to suppertime; come to my table – that, any thing I
have, stands open to thee.

MALEVOLE (To CELSO)
How smooth to him that is in state of grace,
How servile is the rugged'st courtier's face!   75
What Profit, nay, what Nature would keep down,
Are heaved to them, are minions to a crown.
Envious Ambition never sates his thirst,
Till sucking all, he swells, and swells, and bursts.

BILIOSO
I shall now leave you with my always-best wishes; only let's   80
hold betwixt us a firm correspondence, a mutual-friendly-
reciprocal kind of steady-unanimous-heartily-leagued –

MALEVOLE
Did your signiorship ne'er see a pigeon-house that was
smooth, round, and white without, and full of holes and
stink within? Ha' ye not, old courtier?   85

BILIOSO
Oh yes, 'tis the form, the fashion of them all.

---

62 *impart* i.e. you can share why the Duke favours you
65 *possets* hot, spiced drinks of milk curdled with ale or wine
66–71 Bilioso's hint at possible sexual favours from his daughter-in-law and wife is
  amusingly, but puzzlingly, complicated by his digression on the dog.
70 *servant* courtly lover
73 *stands open* is available, with a bawdy quibble
76–7 i.e. those gifts that self-interest and natural modesty or ties of kinship would
  normally repress are freely offered up to those who are royal favourites
81 *correspondence* alliance
83 *pigeon-house* like the 'whited sepulchres' used as a metaphor for hypocrites in
  Matthew xxiii.27

MALEVOLE
Adieu, my true court-friend; farewell, my dear Castilio.

Exit BILIOSO

CELSO (*Descries* MENDOZA)
Yonder's Mendoza.
MALEVOLE   True, the privy key.
CELSO
I take my leave, sweet lord.   *Exit*
MALEVOLE   'Tis fit, away!

[Act I,] Scene v

Enter MENDOZA *with three or four suitors*

MENDOZA
Leave your suits with me; I can and will. Attend my secretary; leave me.

[Exeunt suitors]

MALEVOLE
Mendoza, hark ye, hark ye. You are a treacherous villain,
God b' wi' thee!
MENDOZA
Out, you base-born rascal!   5
MALEVOLE
We are all the sons of Heaven, though a tripe-wife were our
mother. Ah, you whoreson, hot-reined he-marmoset!
Aegisthus, didst ever hear of one Aegisthus?
MENDOZA
'Gisthus?

---

87 *Castilio* A satiric allusion to Baldassare Castiglione, whose *The Book of the
Courtier* was read both as a model of courtesy and a handbook of duplicity and
affectation.
88 s.d. *Descries MENDOZA* who must already be at the stage door with the suitors, so that his 'entrance' below really signals his shift from posturing to speech.
See the Introduction, pp. xxix–xxx.
privy key bawdy pun on his access to the Duke's 'privy-chamber'. The old pronunciation of 'key' as 'kay' forms a couplet with l. 89.

6 *tripe-wife* woman who sells tripe, a lower-class occupation
7 *hot-reined he-marmoset* oversexed monkey; reins = kidneys, understood to be
the seat of sexual desire
8 *Aegisthus* the adulterous lover of Clytemnestra. Their murder of her husband
Agamemnon was revenged by her son Orestes.

MALEVOLE
  Ay, Aegisthus; he was a filthy, incontinent flesh-monger,   10
  such a one as thou art.
MENDOZA
  Out, grumbling rogue!
MALEVOLE
  Orestes, beware Orestes!
MENDOZA
  Out, beggar!
MALEVOLE
  I once shall rise.   15
MENDOZA
  Thou rise?
MALEVOLE
  Ay, at the resurrection.
  No vulgar seed but once may rise, and shall;
  No king so huge but 'fore he die may fall.   *Exit*
MENDOZA
  Now, good Elysium, what a delicious heaven is it for a man   20
  to be in a prince's favour! Oh sweet God! Oh pleasure! Oh
  fortune! Oh all thou best of life! What should I think, what
  say, what do? To be a favourite, a minion! To have a gen-
  eral timorous respect observe a man, a stateful silence in his
  presence, solitariness in his absence, a confused hum and   25
  busy murmur of obsequious suitors training him, the cloth
  held up and way proclaimed before him, petitionary vassals
  licking the pavement with their slavish knees, whilst some
  odd palace-lamprels that engender with snakes and are full
  of eyes on both sides, with a kind of insinuated humbleness,   30
  fix all their delights upon his brow – oh blessed state, what
  a ravishing prospect doth the Olympus of favour yield!
  Death, I cornute the Duke! Sweet women, most sweet
  ladies, nay, angels – by heaven, he is more accursed than a
  devil that hates you, or is hated by you, and happier than a   35
  god that loves you, or is beloved by you! You preservers of

15 *rise* i.e. in social rank
18 *vulgar seed* base person
20–32 Compare Malvolio's daydream of courtly privilege in *Twelfth Night* II.v.44
     ff.
24 *observe* attend
    stateful dignified
26 *training* following
    cloth canopy, carried over dignitaries in procession
29 *lamprels* lampreys, symbols of courtly sycophancy because of their suckers and
    many gill-openings, that looked like eyes

mankind, life-blood of society, who would live, nay, who
can live without you? Oh paradise, how majestical is your
austerer presence! How imperiously chaste is your more
modest face! But oh, how full of ravishing attraction is your   40
pretty, petulant, languishing, lasciviously-composed coun-
tenance: these amorous smiles, those soul-warming,
sparkling glances, ardent as those flames that singed the
world by heedless Phaeton! In body how delicate, in soul
how witty, in discourse how pregnant, in life how wary, in   45
favours how judicious, in day how sociable, and in night
how – oh pleasure unutterable! Indeed, it is most certain
one man cannot deserve only to enjoy a beauteous woman.
But a duchess! In despite of Phoebus, I'll write a sonnet
instantly in praise of her.   *Exit*   50

[Act I,] Scene vi

Enter FERNEZE *ushering* AURELIA, EMILIA *and*
MAQUERELLE *bearing up her train,* BIANCA *attending;*
all go out but AURELIA, MAQUERELLE, *and* FERNEZE

AURELIA
    And is't possible? Mendoza slight me? Possible?
FERNEZE
    Possible!
    What can be strange in him that's drunk with favour,
    Grows insolent with grace? Speak, Maquerelle, speak.

---

39 *austerer presence* the more severe demeanor of chaste modesty, contrasted with
      the enticing behaviour of ll. 40–4
42–4 *these amorous ... Phaeton* Adapted from Quadratus' praise of Meletza to
      Lampatho in Marston's *What You Will* IV.i (*Plays,* ed. Wood, II, 279). In con-
      trast to Quadratus' provocative description, Mendoza's is an example of self-
      intoxication.
44 *Phaeton* son of Apollo, who scorched North Africa and blackened its inhabitants
      when he lost control of the chariot of the sun
44–7 *In body ... unutterable* A trivialized version of Hamlet's praise of mankind's
      god-like qualities (*Hamlet* II.ii.303–7), inviting us to contrast Mendoza's rapture
      with Hamlet's lack of delight.
45 *pregnant* quick-witted
48 *only to enjoy* to enjoy all by himself
49 *Phoebus* the god of poetry

2–3 ed. (one line in Qq)
3 *with favour* Q1–2, Q3 corrected (not in Q3 uncorrected)

MAQUERELLE [*Aside to* FERNEZE]

To speak feelingly, more, more richly in solid sense than   5
worthless words, give me those jewels of your ears to
receive my enforced duty. [*To* AURELIA] As for my part, 'tis
well known I can put up anything, (FERNEZE *privately feeds*
MAQUERELLE'S *hands with jewels during this speech*) can
bear patiently with any man, but when I heard he wronged   10
your precious sweetness, I was enforced to take deep
offence. 'Tis most certain he loves Emilia with high
appetite, and as she told me (as you know we women
impart our secrets one to another), when she repulsed his
suit, in that he was possessed with your endeared grace,   15
Mendoza most ingratefully renounced all faith to you.

FERNEZE

Nay, called you – speak, Maquerelle, speak.

MAQUERELLE

By heaven, 'witch', 'dried biscuit', and contested blushlessly
he loved you but for a spurt or so.

FERNEZE

For maintenance.   20

MAQUERELLE

Advancement and regard.

AURELIA

Oh villain! Oh impudent Mendoza!

MAQUERELLE

Nay, he is the rustiest-jawed, the foulest-mouthed knave in
railing against our sex; he will rail agen' women –

AURELIA

How? How?   25

MAQUERELLE

I am ashamed to speak't, I.

AURELIA

I love to hate him; speak.

MAQUERELLE

Why, when Emilia scorned his base unsteadiness, the black-
throated rascal scolded and said –

AURELIA

What?   30

MAQUERELLE

Troth, 'tis too shameless.

---

8 *put up* Q1 (put Q2–3) endure, with a bawdy quibble repeated in 'bear'
18 *biscuit* Q1, Q3 corrected (bisque Q2, Q3 uncorrected)
19 *spurt* a short time
23 *rustiest-jawed* Q1–2 (rustiest jade Q3) foul-mouthed
24 *agen'* Q1–2 (against Q3)

AURELIA
  What said he?
MAQUERELLE
  Why, that at four women were fools, at fourteen drabs, at
  forty bawds, at fourscore witches, and a hundred, cats.
AURELIA
  O unlimitable impudency!   35
FERNEZE
  But as for poor Ferneze's fixèd heart,
  Was never shadeless meadow drier parched,
  Under the scorching heat of heaven's dog,
  Than is my heart with your enforcing eyes.
MAQUERELLE [*Aside*]
  A hot simile.   40
FERNEZE
  Your smiles have been my heaven, your frowns my hell.
  Oh pity, then; grace should with beauty dwell.
MAQUERELLE [*Aside*]
  Reasonable perfect, by 'r lady!
AURELIA
  I will love thee, be it but in despite
  Of that Mendoza. 'Witch', Ferneze, 'witch'!   45
  Ferneze, thou art the Duchess' favourite:
  Be faithful, private; but 'tis dangerous.
FERNEZE
  His love is lifeless that for love fears breath;
  The worst that's due to sin, oh would 'twere death!
AURELIA
  Enjoy my favour. I will be sick instantly and take physic;   50
  therefore, in depth of night, visit –

33–4 Compare Chapman's *May-Day* (ed. Parrott) III.iii.162–4: 'Where the whore
    ends, the bawd begins, and the corruption of a bawd is the generation of a witch.
    And Pythagoras holds opinion that a witch turns to a wild cat'.
37–9 From a speech by the faithful shepherd Mirtillo in *Il Pastor Fido* II.i, sig. E2v:
    'But never was shadeless meadow dryer parched / Under the baleful fury of the
    heavenly dog / Than was my heart in sunshine of that sweet'.
38 *heaven's dog* Sirius, the dog star, ascendant in July and August
39 *enforcing* compelling
48–9 From the heroine Amarillis' speech in *Il Pastor Fido* III.iv, sig. H3v: 'she loves
    too little that fears death, / Would, gods, death were the worst that's due to sin'.
    In Guarini's play, however, the 'sin' is only violation of arbitrary laws that
    would punish with death lovers who change their beloved, not the adultery
    Ferneze is contemplating.

MAQUERELLE
  Visit her chamber, but conditionally you shall not offend
  her bed – by this diamond!
FERNEZE
  By this diamond. (*Gives it to* MAQUERELLE)
MAQUERELLE
  Nor tarry longer than you please – by this ruby!   55
FERNEZE
  By this ruby. (*Gives again*)
MAQUERELLE
  And that the door shall not creak.
FERNEZE
  And that the door shall not creak.
MAQUERELLE
  Nay, but swear.
FERNEZE
  By this purse. (*Gives her his purse*)   60
MAQUERELLE
  Go to, I'll keep your oaths for you; remember, visit.

                Enter MENDOZA *reading a sonnet*

AURELIA
  'Dried biscuit!' Look where the base wretch comes.
MENDOZA
  'Beauty's life, heaven's model, love's queen,' –
MAQUERELLE
  That's his Emilia.
MENDOZA
  'Nature's triumph, best on earth,' –   65
MAQUERELLE
  Meaning Emilia.
MENDOZA
  'Thou only wonder that the world hath seen!' –
MAQUERELLE
  That's Emilia.
AURELIA
  Must I then hear her praised? Mendoza!
MENDOZA
  Madam, your excellency is graciously encountered: I have   70
  been writing passionate flashes in honour of –
                                        Exit FERNEZE

---

59 MAQUERELLE ed. Assigned to Malevole in Qq.
63–7 Mendoza's poem is derived from Sidney's *Arcadia*, where Pyrocles praises
    Philoclea as 'the ornament of the Earth, the model of Heaven, the Triumph of
    Nature, the light of beauty, Queen of Love' (ed. Feuillerat, I, 90).
71 *flashes* brilliant outbursts

AURELIA

Out, villain, villain!
Oh judgement, where have been my eyes? What
Bewitched election made me dote on thee?
What sorcery made me love thee? But begone;   75
Bury thy head. Oh that I could do more
Than loathe thee! Hence, worst of ill!
No reason ask; our reason is our will.

Exit with MAQUERELLE

MENDOZA

Women? Nay, Furies! – Nay worse, for they torment only
the bad, but women good and bad. Damnation of   80
mankind! Breath, hast thou praised them for this? And is't
you, Ferneze, are wriggled into smock-grace? Sit sure. Oh
that I could rail against these monsters in nature, models of
hell, curse of the earth – women that dare attempt anything,
and what they attempt, they care not how they accomplish: 85
without all premeditation or prevention, rash in asking,
desperate in working, impatient in suffering, extreme in
desiring, slaves unto appetite, mistresses in dissembling,
only constant in unconstancy, only perfect in counterfeit-
ing. Their words are feigned, their eyes forged, their sights   90
dissembled, their looks counterfeit, their hair false, their
given hopes deceitful, their very breath artificial. *Their
blood is their only god; bad clothes and old age are only the
devils they tremble at.* That I could rail now!

72–8 ed. (prose in Qq)

74 *election* choice

78 *ask* Q3 (else Q1–2). Compare Juvenal, VI.223, where an imperious Roman
matron insists on crucifying a slave: '*hoc volo, sic iubeo, sit pro ratione volun-
tas*' ('This I wish, so I command: let my will be my reason').

79–80 *Women … bad* Adapted from Florio, *First Fruites.* See Appendix, 1a.

82 *smock-grace* intimate favour; smock = ladies' shift, undergarment

86 *prevention* precaution

86–8 *rash … desiring* Adapted from Florio, *First Fruites.* See Appendix, 1b.

88 *mistresses* teachers, masters

89–92 *perfect … artificial* Adapted from Guarini, *Il Pastor Fido.* See Appendix, 1c.

90 *sights* sighs (*OED sb²*)

93 *blood* sexual desire

[Act I,] Scene vii

Enter PIETRO, *his sword drawn*

PIETRO
  A mischief fill thy throat, thou foul-jawed slave!
  Say thy prayers.
MENDOZA
  I ha' forgot 'em.
PIETRO
  Thou shalt die.
MENDOZA
  So shalt thou; I am heart-mad.   5
PIETRO
  I am horn-mad.
MENDOZA
  Extreme mad.
PIETRO
  Monstrously mad.
MENDOZA
  Why?
PIETRO
  Why? Thou – thou hast dishonoured my bed.   10
MENDOZA
  I? Come, come, sit; here's my bare heart to thee,
  As steady as is this centre to the glorious world;
  And yet, hark: thou art a *cornuto* – but by me?
PIETRO
  Yes, slave, by thee.
MENDOZA
  Do not, do not with tart and spleenful breath,   15
  Lose him can loose thee. I offend my Duke?
  Bear record, oh ye dumb and raw-aired nights,
  How vigilant my sleepless eyes have been
  To watch the traitor! Record, thou spirit of truth,
  With what debasement I ha' thrown myself   20
  To under-offices, only to learn

---

  6 *horn-mad* enraged like a beast, also 'an angry cuckold'
 11 *sit* Q1–3. Some editors emend to 'sir', but Mendoza may be calling for rational
    discussion at the same time he bares his chest to Pietro's sword.
 12 *centre* the earth, centre of the Ptolemaic universe
 15 *spleenful* irritable
 16 *loose thee* i.e. from your disgrace
 21 *under-offices* menial tasks

The truth, the party, time, the means, the place,
By whom, and when, and where thou wert disgraced!
And am I paid with 'slave'? Hath my intrusion
To places private and prohibited,   25
Only to observe the closer passages –
Heaven knows, with vows of revelation –
Made me suspected, made me deemed a villain?
What rogue hath wronged us?

PIETRO
Mendoza, I may err.   30

MENDOZA
Err! 'Tis too mild a name; but err and err,
Run giddy with suspect, 'fore through me thou know
That which most creatures save thyself do know.
Nay, since my service hath so loathed reject,
'Fore I'll reveal, shalt find them clipped together!   35

PIETRO
Mendoza, thou know'st I am a most plain-breasted man.

MENDOZA
The fitter to make a cuckold. Would your brows were most
plain too!

PIETRO
Tell me; indeed, I heard thee rail –

MENDOZA
At women, true. Why what cold phlegm could choose,   40
Knowing a lord so honest, virtuous,
So boundless-loving, bounteous, fair-shaped, sweet,
To be contemned, abused, defamed, made cuckold!
Heart! I hate all women for't: sweet sheets, wax lights, antic
bed-posts, cambric smocks, villainous curtains, arras pic-   45

26 *closer passages* secret occurrences
27 *vows of revelation* having sworn to reveal everything
32 *'fore* Q1–2 (for Q3)
34 *reject* rejection
35 *clipped* embracing
36 *plain-breasted* simple, honest
37 *cuckold* Q2–3 (cornuto Q1)
40 *cold phlegm* apathetic person; phlegm = one of the four humours or bodily
   fluids believed to determine temperament
44 *sweet* perfumed
   wax cleaner-burning and more expensive than tallow
   antic grotesquely carved
45 *cambric* a fine, soft linen
   arras tapestry, presumably on erotic themes

tures, oiled hinges, and all the tongue-tied lascivious wit-
nesses of great creatures' wantonness! What salvation can
you expect?

PIETRO

Wilt thou tell me?

MENDOZA

Why, you may find it yourself; observe, observe.   50

PIETRO

I ha' not the patience. Wilt thou deserve me? Tell, give it.

MENDOZA

Tak't. Why, Ferneze is the man, Ferneze. I'll prove it; this
night you shall take him in your sheets. Will't serve?

PIETRO

It will; my bosom's in some peace. Till night –

MENDOZA

What?   55

PIETRO

Farewell.

MENDOZA

God! How weak a lord are you!
Why, do you think there is no more but so?

PIETRO

Why?

MENDOZA

Nay, then will I presume to counsel you.   60
It should be thus:
You with some guard upon the sudden break
Into the princess' chamber; I stay behind,
Without the door through which he needs must pass;
Ferneze flies – let him; to me he comes; he's killed   65
By me, observe, by me; you follow; I rail
And seem to save the body. Duchess comes,
On whom (respecting her advancèd birth
And your fair nature) I know – nay, I do know –
No violence must be used. She comes; I storm,   70

---

46 *oiled hinges* to avoid detection of mid-night escapades, a popular subject of
   satire in anti-court drama. Compare *The Revenger's Tragedy* II.ii.140–1 and
   The Atheist's Tragedy (ed. Ribner) I.iv.146, and see Passarello's reference to
   woollen shoes at I.viii.40 below.
   the Q3 (ye Q1–2)

51 *deserve* perform a service worthy of reward

61–3 ed. (It ... suddaine/Breake ... behinde/ Qq)

64 *Without* Outside

68 *advancèd birth* as daughter of the Duke of Florence. See I.iv.19.

I praise, excuse Ferneze, and still maintain
The Duchess' honour; she for this loves me;
I honour you, shall know her soul, you mine;
Then naught shall she contrive in vengeance
(As women are most thoughtful in revenge)   75
Of her Ferneze, but you shall sooner know't
Than she can think't. Thus shall his death come sure,
Your Duchess brain-caught, so your life secure.

PIETRO
It is too well, my bosom and my heart;
When nothing helps, cut off the rotten part.   *Exit*   80

MENDOZA
*Who cannot feign friendship, can ne'er produce the effects
of hatred.* Honest fool Duke, subtle lascivious Duchess,
silly novice Ferneze, I do laugh at ye! My brain is in labour
till it produce mischief; and I feel sudden throes, proofs sensible the issue is at hand: 85
As bears shape young, so I'll form my device,
Which grown, proves horrid; vengeance makes men wise.
                                                 [*Exit*]

[Act I, Scene viii]

Enter MALEVOLE *and* PASSARELLO

MALEVOLE
Fool, most happily encountered! Canst sing, fool?

PASSARELLO
Yes, I can sing, fool, if you'll bear the burden; and I can
play upon instruments, scurvily, as gentlemen do. Oh that I

---

75 *thoughtful* full of schemes
78 *brain-caught* entrapped by deception
81–2 *Who … hatred* From *Il Pastor Fido* II.iv (sig. Fv), where the jealous Corisca
     deceives the heroine Amarillis.
83 *silly* simple, naive
84–5 *sensible* perceptible, evident
86–7 *As bears … horrid* Bears were thought to be unformed at birth and licked into
     shape by their mother. Marston borrows from *Il Pastor Fido* II.iv (sig. I2r),
     where Corisca applies the bear metaphor to the growth of erotic desire into fierce
     passion. Mendoza's version underscores his Machiavellian ruthlessness.

[*Act I, Scene viii*] Addition 4 to Q3, probably by Webster.
  2 *burden* (i) bass accompaniment (ii) responsibility
  3 *scurvily* badly

had been gelded! I should then have been a fat fool for a
chamber, a squeaking fool for a tavern, and a private fool   5
for all the ladies.

MALEVOLE

You are in good case since you came to court, fool; what,
guarded, guarded!

PASSARELLO

Yes, faith, even as footmen and bawds wear velvet, not for
an ornament of honour but for a badge of drudgery; for   10
now the Duke is discontented I am fain to fool him asleep
every night.

MALEVOLE

What are his griefs?

PASSARELLO

He hath sore eyes.

MALEVOLE

I never observed so much.   15

PASSARELLO

Horrible sore eyes; and so hath every cuckold, for the roots
of the horns spring in the eyeballs, and that's the reason the
horn of a cuckold is as tender as his eye, or as that growing
in the woman's forehead twelve years since, that could not
endure to be touched. The Duke hangs down his head like   20
a columbine.

MALEVOLE

Passarello, why do great men beg fools?

PASSARELLO

As the Welshman stole rushes when there was nothing else
to filch: only to keep begging in fashion.

---

4 *gelded* castrated
5 *squeaking* high-voiced
   private intimate, because trusted not to make them pregnant
7 *case* (i) condition (ii) covering, clothes
8 *guarded* ornamented with braid or lace
9 *velvet* Elizabethan sumptuary laws (not always followed) forbade rich fabrics to
   the lower classes.
19 *the woman's forehead* Margaret Griffith of Montgomery, said in a pamphlet of
   1588 to have 'a crooked Horne of four ynches long' growing out of her forehead.
   Webster's date is approximate; see Introduction, p. xiv.
22 *beg fools* The King had custody of idiots and their property, but awarded it to
   courtiers who petitioned and paid a fee.
23 *Welshman* The Welsh were mocked by the Elizabethans for their poverty, their
   language, and for consuming metheglin, cheese, and leeks.

MALEVOLE
Pooh! Thou givest no good reason; thou speakest like a   25
fool.

PASSARELLO
Faith, I utter small fragments as your knight courts your
City widow with jingling of his gilt spurs, advancing his
bush-coloured beard, and taking tobacco. This is all the
mirror of their knightly compliments. Nay, I shall talk   30
when my tongue is a-going once; 'tis like a citizen on horse-
back, evermore in a false gallop.

MALEVOLE
And how doth Maquerelle fare nowadays?

PASSARELLO
Faith, I was wont to salute her as our English women are at
their first landing in Flushing: I would call her whore, but   35
now that antiquity leaves her as an old piece of plastic
t'work by, I only ask her how her rotten teeth fare every
morning and so leave her. She was the first that ever
invented perfumed smocks for the gentlewomen, and
woollen shoes, for fear of creaking, for the visitant. She   40
were an excellent lady, but that her face peeleth like
Muscovy glass.

25 ed. (Pue ... reason,/Thou ... foole/ Q3)
28 *City widow* sought for her former husband's wealth. Webster's allusions to the
   'City' imagine Genoa, like contemporary London within the walls, to be the
   sphere of wealthy merchants and their wives. See the allusion to 'a citizen' at
   l. 31 below.
   jingling ... gilt spurs Q3 corrected (something ... guilt: some Q3 uncorrected)
28–9 *gilt spurs ... tobacco* status-symbols commonly ridiculed in contemporary
   satire
29 *bush-* Q3 corrected (high Q3 uncorrected)
29–30 *This ... compliments* i.e. like Sir Plume in Pope's *The Rape of the Lock*, contemporary knights must use fashionable props to disguise their lack of conver-
   sational ability. Webster also ridicules the popular Spanish romance, *The Mirror
   of Knighthood*.
31–2 *citizen ... false gallop* i.e. a London tradesman, untrained in the knightly art
   of horsemanship, who rides at an awkward gait
34–5 *English women ... in Flushing* England maintained a garrison at this Dutch
   town, women arriving there being welcomed as potential camp-followers.
36 *plastic* any mouldable material
40 *visitant* surreptitious lover who fears detection
42 *Muscovy glass* mica, formed in thin crystalline plates

MALEVOLE

And how doth thy old lord that hath wit enough to be a
flatterer and conscience enough to be a knave?

PASSARELLO

Oh excellent; he keeps beside me fifteen jesters to instruct   45
him in the art of fooling and utters their jests in private to
the Duke and Duchess. He'll lie like to your Switzer or
lawyer: he'll be of any side for most money.

MALEVOLE

I am in haste; be brief.

PASSARELLO

As your fiddler when he is paid. He'll thrive, I warrant you,   50
while your young courtier stands like Good Friday in Lent:
men long to see it because more fatting days come after it;
else he's the leanest and pitifull'st actor in the whole
pageant. Adieu, Malevole.

MALEVOLE

Oh world most vile, when thy loose vanities,   55
Taught by this fool, do make the fool seem wise!

PASSARELLO

You'll know me again, Malevole?

MALEVOLE

Oh, ay, by that velvet.

PASSARELLO

Ay, as a pettifogger by his buckram bag. I am as common
in the court as an hostess' lips in the country: knights, and   60
clowns, and knaves, and all share me; the court cannot
possibly be without me. Adieu, Malevole.

[*Exeunt*]

---

43 *old lord* i.e. Bilioso
47–8 *Switzer or lawyer* The Swiss were noted mercenary soldiers; for lawyers, compare Jonson's reference in *Volpone* I.iii.59–60 to how they 'Give forked counsel;
take provoking gold / On either hand, and put it up'.
52 *fatting days* when eating meat is allowed again
59 *pettifogger ... bag* a lawyer of inferior status, known by his cheap brief-case
61 *me* i.e. folly
62 s.d. ed. (not in Q3)

Act II, Scene i

Enter MENDOZA *with a sconce to observe* FERNEZE's
entrance, who whilst the act is playing, enter[s]
unbraced, two pages before him with lights, is met by
MAQUERELLE, *and conveyed in. The pages are sent*
away

MENDOZA

He's caught; the woodcock's head is i' the noose!
Now treads Ferneze in dangerous path of lust,
Swearing his sense is merely deified.
The fool grasps clouds and shall beget centaurs,
And now in strength of panting faint delight,   5
The goat bids heaven envy him. Good goose,
I can afford thee nothing but the poor
Comfort of calamity, pity.
Lust's like the plummets hanging on clock lines,
Will ne'er ha' done till all is quite undone;   10
Such is the course salt sallow lust doth run,
Which thou shalt try. I'll be revenged. Duke, thy suspect,
Duchess, thy disgrace, Ferneze, thy rivalship,
Shall have swift vengeance. Nothing so holy,
No band of nature so strong,   15
No law of friendship so sacred,
But I'll profane, burst, violate,
'Fore I'll endure disgrace, contempt, and poverty.
Shall I, whose very 'hum' struck all heads bare,

---

 0 s.d. 1 *sconce* lantern
    2 *act* the musical interlude between acts at the Blackfriars Theatre
    3 *unbraced* with doublet and hose unlaced for quicker undress
    4 *pages* Q2–3 (Duchess' pages Q1)
 1 *woodcock* dupe; woodcocks were easily snared
 3 *merely* completely
 4 *fool ... centaurs* the fate of Ixion when he attempted to ravish Juno
 6 *goat* lecher
 7–8 ed. (one line in Qq)
 9 *plummets* the weights whose descent drives the clock
10 *quite undone* Q3 (quite is undone Q1–2)
11 *salt sallow lust* intense, unhealthy lust
12 *try* prove
   suspect jealous suspicion
13 *thy disgrace* i.e. her rejection of Mendoza
19 *whose ... bare* who made everyone doff their hats in respect merely by clearing
   my throat

Whose face made silence, creaking of whose shoe   20
Forced the most private passages fly ope,
Scrape like a servile dog at some latched door?
Learn now to make a leg, and cry 'Beseech ye,
Pray ye, is such a lord within?', be awed
At some odd usher's scoffed formality?   25
First sear my brains! *Unde cadis non quo refert.*
My heart cries, 'Perish all!' How, how! *What fate*
Can once avoid revenge, that's desperate?
I'll to the Duke; if all should ope – if? Tush!
Fortune still dotes on those who cannot blush.   30

[Act II,] Scene ii

Enter MALEVOLE *at one door,* BIANCA, EMILIA, *and*
MAQUERELLE *at the other door*

MALEVOLE
Bless ye, cast o' ladies. Ha, Dipsas, how dost thou, old
coal?
MAQUERELLE
Old coal?
MALEVOLE
Ay, old coal: methinks thou liest like a brand under billets
of green wood. He that will inflame a young wench's heart,   5

---

23 *make a leg* bow
26 *sear* Q1–2, Q3 corrected (seat Q3 uncorrected)
   Unde … refert 'Where you fall from, not to where, matters', Seneca, *Thyestes* ll.
   925–6
27–8 Hunter compares Machiavelli, *Florentine History*: 'It was no part of judgement to drive men into desperation. For whosoever hopeth of no good, feareth
   no evil' (Tudor Translations, p. 86)
30 *cannot blush* i.e. who have no sense of shame, a variation on Virgil, *Aeneid*
   X.284 *'audentes fortuna iuvat'* ('fortune aids the bold')

 1 *cast* handful, pair
   Dipsas Q1–2, Q3 corrected (dip-sawce Q3 uncorrected) the bawd of Ovid,
   Amores I.viii, perhaps named for the serpent whose bite caused unquenchable
   thirst
1–2 *old coal* Compare Overbury's *Characters*: 'A Maquerela, in Plain English, a
   Bawd, Is an old *Char-cole*, that hath been burnt her selfe, and therefore is able
   to kindle a whole green Coppice' (ed. Paylor, p. 42).
 4 *billets* Q3 (these billets Q1–2) i.e. the less experienced Bianca and Emilia

let him lay close to her an old coal that hath first been fired,
a pandress, my half-burnt lint, who though thou canst not
flame thyself, yet art able to set a thousand virgins' tapers
afire. (*To* BIANCA) And how does Janivere thy husband, my
little periwinkle? Is 'a troubled with the cough o' the lungs   10
still? Does he hawk a-nights still? He will not bite.

BIANCA
No, by my troth, I took him with his mouth empty of old
teeth.

MALEVOLE
And he took thee with thy belly full of young bones. Marry,
he took his maim by the stroke of his enemy.   15

BIANCA
And I mine by the stroke of my friend.

MALEVOLE
The close stock! Oh mortal wench! Lady, ha' ye now no
restoratives for your decayed Jasons? Look ye, crabs' guts
baked, distilled ox-pith, the pulverised hairs of a lion's
upper lip, jelly of cock-sparrows, he-monkeys' marrow, or   20
powder of fox-stones. And whither are all you ambling
now?

BIANCA
Why, to bed, to bed.

MALEVOLE
Do your husbands lie with ye?

BIANCA
That were country fashion, i' faith.   25

---

7 *lint* used as tinder
  canst not Q1–2, Q3 corrected (canst Q3 uncorrected)
9 s.d. Q2 (not in Q1, 3)
  does Q1–2 (doth Q3)
  Janivere January, the old husband with a young, unfaithful wife in Chaucer's
  Merchant's Tale
10 *Is 'a* Q1–2 (Is he Q3)
17 *close stock* secret thrust; stock = *stoccado*, a fencing term
18 *restoratives ... Jasons* Medea restored the youth of Jason's father Aeson; the
  ingredients Malevole lists were considered aphrodisiacs
21 *fox-stones* fox testicles
  all you Q1–2 (you Q3)
23 *Why,* Q1–2 (not in Q3)
25 *country fashion* rude, unsophisticated (aristocratic couples usually had separate
  bedchambers). Compare the Ladies Collegiates' criticism of Morose for his 'mere
  rusticity' in Jonson's *Epicoene*, III.vi.76.

MALEVOLE
Ha' ye no foregoers about you? Come, whither in good
deed, la now?
BIANCA
In good indeed, la now, to eat the most miraculously,
admirably, astonishable-composed posset with three curds,
without any drink. Will ye help me with a he-fox? Here's   30
the Duke.

The ladies go out

MALEVOLE (*To* BIANCA)
Fried frogs are very good, and French-like too.

[Act II,] Scene iii

Enter Duke PIETRO, *Count* CELSO, *Count* EQUATO,
BILIOSO, FERRARDO, *and* MENDOZA

PIETRO
The night grows deep and foul. What hour is't?
CELSO
Upon the stroke of twelve.
MALEVOLE
Save ye, Duke!
PIETRO
From thee. Begone, I do not love thee; let me see thee no
more; we are displeased.   5
MALEVOLE
Why, God b' wi' thee. Heaven, hear my curse:
May thy wife and thee live long together.
PIETRO
Begone, sirrah!
MALEVOLE [*Sings*]
'When Arthur first in court began' – Agamemnon –
Menelaus – was ever any duke a *cornuto*?   10

26 *foregoers* gentlemen-ushers
28–31 Assigned to Maquerelle in Q1–2, Bianca in Q3.
29–30 *three ... drink* curdled in three layers without whey, or perhaps made with-
    out ale, using only the 'restorative' ingredients listed at II.iv.8–14
32 Q3 (not in Q1–2)

4 *From thee* i.e. protect me from the likes of you
6 *b' wi' thee* ed. (buy thee Q1–2; be with thee Q3)
9 '*When ... began*' first line of a ballad sung by Falstaff in 2 *Henry IV* II.iv; like
    Agamemnon and Menelaus, Arthur was a famous cuckold

PIETRO
  Begone hence!
MALEVOLE
  What religion wilt thou be of next?
MENDOZA
  Out with him!
MALEVOLE [*To* PIETRO]
  With most servile patience, time will come
  When wonder of thy error will strike dumb   15
  Thy bezzled sense.
  Slaves i' favour! Ay marry, shall he rise?
                                  [*Pointing to* MENDOZA]
  Good God! How subtle Hell doth flatter Vice,
  Mounts him aloft, and makes him seem to fly,
  As fowl the tortoise mocked, who to the sky   20
  The ambitious shell-fish raised: th'end of all
  Is only that from height he might dead fall.
BILIOSO
  Why, when? Out, ye rogue! Begone, ye rascal!
MALEVOLE
  I shall now leave ye with all my best wishes.
BILIOSO
  Out, ye cur!   25
MALEVOLE
  'Only let's hold together a firm correspondence' –
BILIOSO
  Out!
MALEVOLE
  'A mutual-friendly-reciprocal-perpetual kind of steady-
  unanimous-heartily-leagued' –
BILIOSO
  Hence, ye gross-jawed, peasantly – out, go!   30
MALEVOLE
  Adieu, pigeon-house! Thou burr that only stickest to nappy

12 i.e. Pietro has changed his 'faith' in Malevole
16–17 ed. (one line in Q1–3)
16 *bezzled* befuddled (with drinking)
17 *i' favour!* ed. (I favour, Qq)
    shall he rise? ed. (shall he rise, Q1; shall he, rise, Q2–3)
19 *Mounts* Q3 (mount Q1–2)
20–2 *As fowl ... fall* Compare Sidney, *Arcadia*: '... exalting him only to his over-
    throw; like the bird that carries the shell-fish high, to break him easier with his
    fall' (ed. Feuillerat, I, 330), derived from Pliny, *Natural History* X.iii.7.
23–37 Addition 5 to Q3, probably by Marston.
26–9 Repeating Bilioso's words from I.iv.80–2.
31 *nappy* shaggy, with a deep pile, and thus rich

fortunes, the serpigo, the strangury, an eternal, uneffectual
priapism seize thee!

BILIOSO

Out, rogue!

MALEVOLE

May'st thou be a notorious, wittolly pander to thine own   35
wife and yet get no office, but live to be the utmost misery
of mankind, a beggarly cuckold.   *Exit*

PIETRO [*To* MENDOZA]

It shall be so.

MENDOZA

It must be so, *for where great states revenge,*
'Tis requisite the parts which piety   40
And loft respect forbears be closely dogged;
Lay one into his breast shall sleep with him,
Feed in the same dish, run in self faction,
Who may discover any shape of danger;
For once disgraced, displayèd in offence,   45
It makes man blushless, and man is (all confess)
More prone to vengeance than to gratefulness.
Favours are writ in dust, but stripes we feel;
Depravèd nature stamps in lasting steel.

PIETRO

You shall be leagued with the Duchess.   50

EQUATO

The plot is very good.

---

32 *serpigo* skin infection, herpes
    strangury painful urination
33 *priapism* persistent erection
35 *wittolly* agreeable. A wittol was one who foolishly ignored his wife's infidelity.
39–41 *where ... dogged* where a prince takes revenge, it is necessary that those who
    dispense with duty or respect to the great be closely watched
40 *which* ed. (with Qq)
42–4 Compare Ferdinand's recruitment of Bosola as a spy in Webster's *The
    Duchess of Malfi* I.i.280–5. Mendoza is volunteering to play such a role for
    Pietro.
43 *run ... faction* join the same clique or conspiracy
44 *discover* Q2–3 (dissever Q1)
45 *displayèd* Q2–3 (discovered Q1)
46 *blushless* shameless. Mendoza correctly anticipates that Aurelia's response to her
    exposure will be to seek revenge.
46–7 *man ... gratefulness* Compare R. Dallington, *Aphorisms* (1613), p. 208.
48–9 Compare Sir John Harrington's translation of Ariosto, *Orlando Furioso* (ed.
    McNulty), XXIII, 1: 'Good turns in sand, shrewd turns are writ in brass'.

PIETRO
    You shall both kill, and seem the corse to save.
FERRARDO
    A most fine brain-trick.
CELSO (*Tacite*)   Of a most cunning knave.
PIETRO
    My lords, the heavy action we intend
    Is death and shame, two of the ugliest shapes   55
    That can confound a soul; think, think of it.
    I strike, but yet like him that 'gainst stone walls
    Directs his shafts, rebounds in his own face,
    My lady's shame is mine; oh God, 'tis mine!
    Therefore, I do conjure all secrecy;   60
    Let it be as very little as may be –
    Pray ye, as may be.
    Make frightless entrance, salute her with soft eyes,
    Stain nought with blood – only Ferneze dies,
    But not before her brows. Oh gentlemen,   65
    God knows I love her! Nothing else, but this:
    I am not well. If grief, that sucks veins dry,
    Rivels the skin, casts ashes in men's faces,
    Bedulls the eye, unstrengthens all the blood,
    Chance to remove me to another world –   70
    As sure I once must die – let him succeed.
    I have no child; all that my youth begot
    Hath been your loves, which shall inherit me;
    Which, as it ever shall, I do conjure it
    Mendoza may succeed: he's noble born,   75
    With me of much desert.
CELSO (*Tacite*)
    Much!
PIETRO
    Your silence answers 'ay';
    I thank you. Come on, now. Oh that I might die
    Before her shame's displayed! Would I were forced   80

---

52 *PIETRO* ed. Qq give this speech to Mendoza, but since it describes his own acts,
    the compositor may have confused his name in the text, which would fill out the
    previous half-line, with the speech-heading.
    corse corpse (course Qq)
53, 77 s.d. *Tacite* Silently, aside
60 *conjure* implore
64 *Stain* Q1, Q3 corrected (Strain Q2, Q3 uncorrected)
65 *before ... brows* before her eyes
68 *Rivels* Wrinkles
71 *him* i.e. Mendoza
75 *noble* Q2–3 (nobly Q1)

To burn my father's tomb, unhele his bones,
And dash them in the dirt, rather than this!
This both the living and the dead offends:
Sharp surgery where nought but death amends.

Exit with the others

[Act II,] Scene iv

Enter MAQUERELLE, EMILIA, *and* BIANCA *with the posset*

MAQUERELLE
Even here it is – three curds in three regions individually
distinct, most methodically according to art composed,
without any drink.

BIANCA
Without any drink?

MAQUERELLE
Upon my honour. Will ye sit and eat?   5

EMILIA
Good, the composure, the receipt, how is't?

MAQUERELLE [*Inviting* EMILIA *to give her a jewel*]
'Tis a pretty pearl; by this pearl (how dost with me?), thus
it is: seven and thirty yolks of Barbary hens' eggs; eighteen
spoonfuls and a half of the juice of cocksparrow bones; one
ounce, three drams, four scruples, and one quarter of the   10
syrup of Ethiopian dates; sweetened with three quarters of
a pound of pure candied Indian eringoes; strewed over with
the powder of pearl of America, amber of Cataia, and
lamb-stones of Muscovia.

BIANCA
Trust me, the ingredients are very cordial, and no question   15
good, and most powerful in restoration.

---

81 *unhele* Q3 (unhill Q1–2) uncover

 2 *methodically* Q1–2 (methodical Q3). An ambiguous line whose preferred read-
     ing will depend on whether 'methodical(ly)' is seen as modifying what precedes
     or follows it.

 5 *ye* Q1–2 (you Q3)

 6 *composure* recipe

 7 *how ... me?* how does it look on me?

10 *scruple* one twenty-fourth of an ounce. This recipe is 'methodical' indeed!

12 *eringoes* sea-holly roots, considered an aphrodisiac

13 *amber of Cataia* ambergris from China

14 *lamb-stones* lamb's testicles

MAQUERELLE

I know not what you mean by 'restoration', but this it doth:
it purifieth the blood, smootheth the skin, enliveneth the
eye, strengtheneth the veins, mundifieth the teeth, com-
forteth the stomach, fortifieth the back, and quickeneth the   20
wit; that's all.

EMILIA

By my troth, I have eaten but two spoonfuls, and methinks
I could discourse most swiftly and wittily already.

MAQUERELLE

Have you the art to seem honest?

BIANCA

I thank advice and practice.   25

MAQUERELLE

Why then, eat me o' this posset, quicken your blood, and
preserve your beauty. Do you know Doctor Plaster-face?
By this curd, he is the most exquisite in forging of veins,
sprightening of eyes, dyeing of hair, sleeking of skins,
blushing of cheeks, surfling of breasts, blanching and   30
bleaching of teeth that ever made an old lady gracious by
torchlight; by this curd, la.

BIANCA

Well, we are resolved; what God has given us we'll cherish.

MAQUERELLE

Cherish anything saving your husband; keep him not too
high, lest he leap the pale. But for your beauty, let it be your   35
saint; bequeath two hours to it every morning in your
closet. I ha' been young, and yet in my conscience I am not
above five and twenty, but believe me, preserve and use
your beauty; for youth and beauty once gone, we are like
beehives without honey, out-o'-fashion apparel that no   40
man will wear; therefore use me your beauty.

EMILIA

Ay, but men say –

MAQUERELLE

Men say! Let men say what the' will! Life o' woman, they

---

19 *mundifieth* cleans

26 *o' this* Q1–2 (of this Q3)

28 *forging of veins* painting artificial veins over the cosmetic base

30 *surfling* painting with sulphur-water or cosmetics

33 *Well* Q1–2 (We Q3)

34–5 *keep ... pale* (i) don't give him such rich food that he has an excess of sexual
energy, or (ii) don't gratify his desire so much that he tires of you sexually
pale fence

35–49 Adapted from *Il Pastor Fido*. See Appendix, 2.

43 *the'* Q1–2 (they Q3)

are ignorant of our wants: the more in years, the more in
perfection the' grow. If they lose youth and beauty, they   45
gain wisdom and discretion, but when our beauty fades,
goodnight with us! There cannot be an uglier thing to see
than an old woman, from which, oh pruning, pinching and
painting, deliver all sweet beauties.

[Music within]

BIANCA
Hark, music.   50
MAQUERELLE
Peace, 'tis i' the Duchess' bedchamber. Good rest, most
prosperously-graced ladies.
EMILIA
Goodnight, sentinel.
BIANCA
'Night, dear Maquerelle.

Exeunt all but MAQUERELLE

MAQUERELLE
May my posset's operation send you my wit and honesty,   55
and me your youth and beauty. The pleasingest rest! *Exit*

[Act II,] Scene v

A song

Whilst the song is singing, enter MENDOZA *with his
sword drawn, standing ready to murder* FERNEZE *as he
flies from the Duchess' chamber*

ALL [*Within*]
Strike, strike!

44 *our* Q1–2 (your Q3)
45 *the'* Q1–2 (they Q3)
48–9 *from ... beauties* Maquerelle parodies the Book of Common Prayer and
    inverts the ending of Jonson's *Cynthia's Revels*, where Mercury leads the
    courtiers in renouncing 'pargeting, painting, slicking, glazing, and renewing old
    rivelled faces' ('Palinode', ll. 22–3).
51 *i' the* Q1–2 (in the Q3)
54 s.d. Q2–3 (*Exeunt at several doors* Q1)

1 s.d. from margin of Q1–2 (not in Q3)

[*Tumult within*]

AURELIA [*Within*]
  Save my Ferneze! Oh save my Ferneze!

Enter FERNEZE *in his shirt, and is received upon*
MENDOZA'S *sword*

ALL [*Within*]
  Follow! Pursue!
AURELIA [*Within*]
  Oh save Ferneze!
MENDOZA
  Pierce, pierce!

Thrusts his rapier in FERNEZE

  Thou shallow fool, drop there.   5
He that attempts a princess' lawless love
Must have broad hands, close heart, with Argus' eyes,
And back of Hercules, or else he dies.

Enter AURELIA, *Duke* PIETRO, FERRARDO, BILIOSO,
CELSO, *and* EQUATO

ALL
  Follow! Follow!

MENDOZA *bestrides the wounded body of* FERNEZE *and*
seems to save him

MENDOZA
  Stand off! Forbear, ye most uncivil lords!   10
PIETRO
  Strike!
MENDOZA Do not; tempt not a man resolved.
  Would you, inhuman murderers, more than death?
AURELIA
  Oh poor Ferneze!
MENDOZA
  Alas, now all defence too late.
AURELIA   He's dead!   15

5 s.d. Q2–3, where it follows l. 8 (not in Q1)
6–8 Compare *The Fawn* (ed. Smith) III.i.510–11: 'For 'tis of knowing creatures the
  main art / To use quick hams, wide arms, and most close heart'.
6 *princess'* ed. (princes Qq)
7 *Argus' eyes* Argos Panoptes, the guardian of Io, had eyes all over his body.
8 *back of Hercules* i.e. both strength and sexual endurance. See IV.v.58–61n.
9 s.d. from margin of Q1–2 (not in Q3)

PIETRO
  I am sorry for our shame. Go to your bed;
  Weep not too much, but leave some tears to shed
  When I am dead.
AURELIA
  What, weep for thee? My soul no tears shall find.
PIETRO
  Alas, alas, that women's souls are blind.   20
MENDOZA
  Betray such beauty!
  Murder such youth! Contemn civility!
  He loves him not that rails not at him.
PIETRO
  Thou canst not move us; we have blood enough.
  And please you, lady, we have quite forgot   25
  All your defects; if not, why then –
AURELIA   Not.
PIETRO   Not.
  The best of rest. Goodnight.

                    Exit PIETRO *with other courtiers*

AURELIA   Despite go with thee!
MENDOZA
  Madam, you ha' done me foul disgrace!
  You have wronged him much loves you too much.
  Go to; your soul knows you have.   30
AURELIA
  I think I have.
MENDOZA
  Do you but think so?
AURELIA
  Nay, sure I have; my eyes have witnessed thy love:
  Thou hast stood too firm for me.
MENDOZA
  Why tell me, fair-cheeked lady, who even in tears   35
  Art powerfully beauteous, what unadvisèd passion
  Struck ye into such a violent heat against me?

21–2 ed. (one line in Qq)
23 i.e. whoever does not condemn such actions does not have Pietro's best interest
    at heart
24 *move us* make us angry
25 *And* If it
26–7 ed. (prose in Qq)
29 *loves* who loves

Speak: what mischief wronged us? What devil injured us?
Speak.

AURELIA
That thing ne'er worthy of the name of man – Ferneze.   40
Ferneze swore thou lov'st Emilia,
Which to advance with most reproachful breath,
Thou both didst blemish and denounce my love.

MENDOZA
Ignoble villain, did I for this bestride
Thy wounded limbs – for this? – rank opposite   45
Even to my sovereign – for this? Oh God, for this!
Sunk all my hopes, and with my hopes my life,
Ripped bare my throat unto the hangman's axe –
Thou most dishonoured trunk! – Emilia?
By life, I know her not – Emilia!   50
Did you believe him?   Pardon me, I did.

AURELIA

MENDOZA
Did you? And thereupon you graced him?

AURELIA   I did.

MENDOZA
Took him to favour, nay, even clasped with him?

AURELIA
Alas, I did.

MENDOZA
This night?   55

AURELIA
This night.

MENDOZA
And in your lustful twines the Duke took you?

AURELIA
A most sad truth.

MENDOZA
Oh God, oh God! How we dull honest souls,
Heavy-brained men, are swallowed in the bogs   60
Of a deceitful ground, whilst nimble bloods,
Light-jointed spirits, pent, cut good men's throats

45–6 *for ... sovereign* Q1–2 (not in Q3). I follow the speech rhythm as punctuated
    in Q1–2; most editors regroup the words (limbs? for this rank ... sovereign? for
    this ... sunk all my hopes?), but the speech makes sense as originally printed.
45 *rank opposite* stand in opposition
49 *trunk* corpse
53 *clasped with* had intercourse with
62 *Light-jointed spirits, pent* ed. (light-jointed spirits pent, Q1–2; light-jointed spir-
    its spent, Q3) *pent* = penned in. Mendoza mixes two different metaphors for

And scape! Alas, I am too honest for this age,
Too full of phlegm and heavy steadiness,
Stood still whilst this slave cast a noose about me;   65
Nay, then to stand in honour of him and her,
Who had even sliced my heart!

AURELIA   Come, I did err
And am most sorry I did err.

MENDOZA
Why we are both but dead; the Duke hates us,
And those whom princes do once groundly hate,   70
Let them provide to die, as sure as fate;
Prevention is the heart of policy.

AURELIA
Shall we murder him?

MENDOZA
Instantly?

AURELIA
Instantly, before he casts a plot,   75
Or further blaze my honour's much-known blot,
Let's murder him.

MENDOZA
I would do much for you; will ye marry me?

AURELIA
I'll make thee Duke: we are of Medicis,
Florence our friend, in court my faction   80
Not meanly strengthful; the Duke then dead,

---

entrapment to contrast his own pretended honesty with those who escape from
tight situations by amoral ruthlessness. Hunter follows Q3 and emends the punctuation to 'light-jointed, spirits spent', but this makes the last phrase contradict
'nimble bloods'; the reading of Q1–2 seems preferable as emended.

64 *full of phlegm* i.e. slow to become indignant

66 *to stand in honour of* to fight for the honour of

67–8 ed. (Who ... heart./Come ... erre/ Qq)

70–2 Hunter compares Sidney's 'Old' *Arcadia* (ed. Feuillerat, IV, 146): 'whosoever
hath thoroughly offended a prince can never think itself in perfect safety under
him'.

70 *groundly* with good reason, thoroughly

71 *provide* prepare

72 i.e. political cunning dictates that we kill him before he kills us; prevention =
anticipation

74–5 Q1–2 (Instantly./Instantly? before he casts a plot? Q3)

76 *blaze* display, as on an heraldic shield or blazon

79 *we ... Medicis* i.e. My father is the Medici Duke of Florence (see I.iv.19).
Marston exploits the reputation of the Medicis for Machiavellian intrigue.

81 *not meanly* not moderately, i.e. very

We well prepared for change, the multitude
Irresolutely reeling, we in force,
Our party seconded, the kingdom mazed –
No doubt of swift success all shall be graced.   85
MENDOZA
You do confirm me; we are resolute;
Tomorrow look for change, rest confident.
'Tis now about the immodest waist of night;
The mother of moist dew with pallid light
Spreads gloomy shades about the numbèd earth.   90
Sleep, sleep, whilst we contrive our mischief's birth.
This man I'll get inhumed. Farewell, to bed;
Ay, kiss thy pillow, dream, the Duke is dead.
So, so, goodnight.

                                                  Exit AURELIA

How Fortune dotes on impudence!   95
I am in private the adopted son
Of yon good prince. I must be Duke. Why, if
I must, I must! Most silly lord, name me?
Oh heaven! I see God made honest fools
To maintain crafty knaves. The Duchess is wholly   100
Mine, too: must kill her husband to quit
Her shame – much! – Then marry her. Ay!
Oh, I grow proud in prosperous treachery!
As wrestlers clip, so I'll embrace you all,
Not to support, but to procure your fall.   105

                           Enter MALEVOLE

MALEVOLE
God arrest thee!
MENDOZA
At whose suit?

---

84 *mazed* stunned, bewildered
85 *success all* Q1–2 (success, all Q3) i.e. undoubtedly everything shall be graced
   with swift success
88 *waist* middle. Compare *Hamlet* II.ii.232–6 and *Measure for Measure* IV.i.34–5.
92 *inhumed* buried
93 ed. 'I kiss thy pillow, dream, the Duke is dead.' Q1–2 (kiss the Q3). The quartos regularly use 'I' for both 'I' and 'ay', creating an ambiguity here.
94–102 ed. (So ... impudence/I ... Prince/I ... must/Most ... heaven/I ... knaves/
   The ... husband/To ... I/ Qq)
98 *silly* simple, senseless
104 *clip* hug

MALEVOLE

At the Devil's. Ha, you treacherous, damnable monster!
How dost? How dost, thou treacherous rogue? Ha, ye
rascal, I am banished the court, sirrah.   110

MENDOZA

Prithee, let's be acquainted; I do love thee, faith.

MALEVOLE

At your service, by the Lord, la! Shall's go to supper? Let's
be once drunk together, and so unite a most virtuously
strengthened friendship; shall's, Huguenot, shall's?

MENDOZA

Wilt fall upon my chamber tomorrow morn?   115

MALEVOLE

As a raven to a dunghill. They say there's one dead here,
pricked for the pride of the flesh.

MENDOZA

Ferneze. There he is; prithee, bury him.

MALEVOLE

O most willingly; I mean to turn pure Rochelle churchman,
I.   120

MENDOZA

Thou churchman! Why? Why?

MALEVOLE

Because I'll live lazily, rail upon authority, deny kings'
supremacy in things indifferent, and be a Pope in mine own
parish.

MENDOZA

Wherefore dost thou think churches were made?   125

MALEVOLE

To scour ploughshares. I ha' seen oxen plough up altars. *Et
nunc seges ubi Sion fuit.*

108, 109 *Ha* Q1–2 (Ah Q3)

110 *sirrah* a term of contempt

114 *Huguenot* literally 'comrade', the name for French Calvinists, here taken as a
    type for hypocrisy

117 *pride* lust, desire

118 *prithee* Q3 (prey thee Q1–2)

119 *Rochelle* a haven for French Huguenots; but Malevole is really satirising English
    Puritans

122–4 *deny ... parish* Puritan clergy claimed exemption from liturgical practices to
    which they objected on the grounds that the King, head of the Anglican Church,
    had no authority to dictate matters not essential to salvation, thus reserving
    decisions on such issues to their own pastoral authority.

126 *ha' seen* Q1–2 (have seen Q3)

126–7 *Et ... fuit* 'And now there is a cornfield where Sion was', adapted from Ovid,

MENDOZA
  Strange!
MALEVOLE
  Nay, monstrous! I ha' seen a sumptuous steeple turned to a
  stinking privy; more beastly, the sacred'st place made a   130
  dog's kennel; nay, most inhuman, the stoned coffins of long
  dead Christians burst up and made hog's troughs – *Hic finis*
  Priami. Shall I ha' some sack and cheese at thy chamber?
  Goodnight, good mischievous, incarnate devil; goodnight,
  Mendoza. Ha, ye inhuman villain, goodnight; 'night, fub!   135
MENDOZA
  Goodnight. Tomorrow morn?   *Exit*
MALEVOLE
  Ay, I will come, friendly damnation, I will come. I do
  descry cross-points; honesty and courtship straddle as far
  asunder as a true Frenchman's legs.
FERNEZE
  Oh!   140
MALEVOLE
  Proclamations, more proclamations!
FERNEZE
  Oh, a surgeon!
MALEVOLE
  Hark, lust cries for a surgeon. What news from Limbo?
  How does the grand cuckold, Lucifer?
FERNEZE
  Oh help, help! Conceal and save me!   145

        FERNEZE *stirs, and* MALEVOLE *helps him up and*
                    conveys him away

'*Iam seges est ubi Troia fuit*', *Heroides*, l. 53. Marston seems to be glancing at
the destruction of church property after the Reformation.
132–3 *Hic finis Priami* 'Such is the end of Priam', adapted from Virgil, *Aeneid*, II.554
133 *sack* sherry wine
135 *Ha, ye* Q1–2 (Ah, you Q3)
     fub cheat
138 *cross-points* fancy dance-steps, trickery
     courtship courtiership
138–9 *straddle ... legs* as the walk of those afflicted with the 'French' pox was under-
     stood to be affected. Compare Marston's reference to the 'true French pestilence'
     in *The Scourge of Villainie* III.94.
143 *Limbo* the underworld, as if he were returning from the dead
144 *does* Q1–2 (doth Q3)

MALEVOLE

Thy shame more than thy wounds do grieve me far;
Thy wounds but leave upon thy flesh some scar,
But fame ne'er heals, still rankles worse and worse;
Such is of uncontrollèd lust the curse.
Think what it is in lawless sheets to lie,   150
But oh, Ferneze, what in lust to die!
Then thou that shame respects, oh fly converse
With women's eyes, and lisping wantonness.
Stick candles 'gainst a virgin wall's white back:
If they not burn, yet at the least, they'll black.   155
Come, I'll convey thee to a private port,
Where thou shalt live (oh happy man) from court.
The beauty of the day begins to rise,
From whose bright form night's heavy shadow flies;
Now 'gins close plots to work; the scene grows full,   160
And craves his eyes who hath a solid skull.

Exeunt

Act III, Scene i

Enter Duke PIETRO, MENDOZA, *Count* EQUATO, *and*
BILIOSO

PIETRO

'Tis grown to youth of day; how shall we waste this light?
My heart's more heavy than a tyrant's crown.
Shall we go hunt? Prepare for field.

Exit EQUATO

MENDOZA

Would ye could be merry.

PIETRO

Would God I could! Mendoza, bid 'em haste.   5

Exit MENDOZA

---

146 *do grieve* This seems to need emendation, but the line's syntax is ambiguous, and
    I follow all other editors in leaving it stand.

148 *fame* ill repute

152 *converse* familiarity

156 *port* refuge

157 *from* away from

161 *craves ... skull* requires observation by someone with a sharp mind

I would fain shift place – oh vain relief!
Sad souls may well change place, but not change grief;
As deer, being struck, fly thorough many soils,
Yet still the shaft sticks fast, so –
BILIOSO
A good old simile, my honest lord.   10
PIETRO
I am not much unlike to some sick man
That long desirèd hurtful drink; at last
Swills in and drinks his last, ending at once
Both life and thirst. Oh, would I ne'er had known
My own dishonour! Good God, that men should   15
Desire to search out that which, being found, kills all
Their joy of life! To taste the tree of knowledge
And then be driven from out paradise!
Canst give me some comfort?
BILIOSO
My lord, I have some books which have been dedicated to   20
my honour, and I ne'er read 'em, and yet they had very fine
names: *Physic for Fortune, Lozenges of Sanctified Sincerity*,
very pretty works of curates, scriveners, and schoolmasters.
Marry, I remember one Seneca, Lucius Annaeus Seneca –
PIETRO
Out upon him! He writ of temperance and fortitude, yet   25
lived like a voluptuous epicure, and died like an effeminate
coward. Haste thee to Florence.
Here, take our letters, see 'em sealed; away!
Report in private to the honoured Duke

---

7 Compare Horace, *Epistles* I.xi.27: '*coelum non animam mutant qui trans mare
   currunt*' ('those who cross the sea change the sky, not their soul').

8–9 *As deer ... fast* Adapted from Virgil, *Aeneid* IV.69–73.

8 *soils* pools or watery places

9 *sticks* Q3 (stick Q1–2)

10 *BILIOSO* Q3 (*MENDOZA* Q2; assigned to Pietro in Q1)

11–14 From *Il Pastor Fido* III.vi (sig. I2), where it is spoken by Mirtillo after he
   finally obtains an interview with Amarillis, only to be rejected by her.

17–18 *To taste ... paradise* Pietro's experience has recapitulated the fall of mankind
   in Genesis ii–iii.

22 *Physic for Fortune, Lozenges of Sanctified Sincerity* The first title recalls Thomas
   Twynne's *Physic against Fortune*, translated from Petrarch; the second is a satiric
   hit at popular books of piety like Thomas Becon's *The Pomander of Prayer*.

25–7 *Out ... coward* The former tutor of Nero, the wealthy Seneca led a comfort-
   able life until forced to commit suicide by the emperor. He cut his wrists in a
   warm bath.

28–32 ed. (prose in Qq)

His daughter's forced disgrace. Tell him at length   30
We know too much; due compliments advance:
There's naught that's safe and sweet but ignorance.   *Exit*

Enter BIANCA

BILIOSO

Madam, I am going ambassador for Florence; 'twill be
great charges to me.

BIANCA

No matter, my lord, you have the lease of two manors   35
come out next Christmas; you may lay your tenants on the
greater rack for it, and when you come home again, I'll
teach you how you shall get two hundred pounds a year by
your teeth.

BILIOSO

How, madam?   40

BIANCA

Cut off so much from housekeeping: that which is saved by
the teeth, you know, is got by the teeth.

BILIOSO

'Fore God, and so I may; I am in wondrous credit, lady.

BIANCA

See the use of flattery; I did ever counsel you to flatter greatness, and you have profited well. Any man that will do so   45
shall be sure to be like your Scotch barnacle: now a block,
instantly a worm, and presently a great goose. This it is to
rot and putrefy in the bosom of greatness.

BILIOSO

Thou art ever my politician. Oh how happy is that old lord

---

31 *compliments* Q2–3 (complaints Q1) courtly courtesies

32 A bitter version of Erasmus' *Adages*, II.x.81, derived from Sophocles' *Ajax*, l.
554, that 'In knowing nothing is the sweetest life', *Collected Works of Erasmus
in English*, 34 (1992).

32 s.d.–145 Addition 6, probably by Webster.

32 s.d. ed. (*Enter* BILIOSO *and* BIANCA Q3). Bilioso is already on-stage.

34 *charges* expenses

36 *come out* expire (and so allow rents to be raised)

41 *housekeeping* Traditionally, great landowners kept 'open house' in their great
halls, feeding their tenants and the neighbourhood poor; the decline of the practice due to inflationary pressures in the Jacobean period was criticised as a failure of social responsibility.

43 *credit* favour with the Duke

46 *Scotch barnacle* Reported in Chapter 188 of Gerard's *Herbal* (1597) to grow on
trees by the seaside and become geese upon falling into the water.

49 *politician* shrewd schemer

that hath a politician to his young lady! I'll have fifty　50
gentlemen shall attend upon me; marry, the most of them
shall be farmers' sons because they shall bear their own
charges, and they shall go apparelled thus: in sea-water-
green suits, ash-colour cloaks, watchet stockings, and
popinjay-green feathers. Will not the colours do excellent?　55

BIANCA
Out upon't! They'll look like citizens riding to their friends
at Whitsuntide, their apparel just so many several parishes.

BILIOSO
I'll have it so, and Passarello, my fool, shall go along with
me; marry, he shall be in velvet.

BIANCA
A fool in velvet?　60

BILIOSO
Ay, 'tis common for your fool to wear satin; I'll have mine
in velvet.

BIANCA
What will you wear, then, my lord?

BILIOSO
Velvet, too; marry, it shall be embroidered, because I'll
differ from the fool somewhat. I am horribly troubled with　65
the gout; nothing grieves me but that my doctor hath forbidden me wine, and you know your ambassador must
drink. Didst thou ask thy doctor what was good for the
gout?

BIANCA
Yes; he said ease, wine, and women were good for it.　70

BILIOSO
Nay, thou hast such a wit! What was good to cure it, said
he?

BIANCA
Why, the rack. All your empirics could never do the like

50–1 *fifty gentlemen* Though increasingly difficult to maintain, a 'train' of retainers
or backers was still a desirable symbol of status among the nobility, but the joke
here is that these upwardly-mobile farmers' sons will hardly comprise an
impressive retinue.

54 *watchet* light blue

57 *Whitsuntide* the seventh Sunday after Easter, when the weather was warm
enough for excursions

their ... parishes a jumble of clashing colours, like those on a map

59, 61 *velvet, satin* fabrics normally reserved for those of high status in contemporary sumptuary laws

cure upon the gout the rack did in England, or your Scotch
boot. The French harlequin will instruct you.   75

BILIOSO
Surely I do wonder how thou, having for the most part of
thy lifetime been a country body, shouldst have so good a
wit.

BIANCA
Who, I? Why, I have been a courtier thrice two months.

BILIOSO
So have I this twenty year, and yet there was a gentleman-   80
usher called me cockscomb t'other day, and to my face, too.
Was't not a back-biting rascal? I would I were better travelled, that I might have been better acquainted with the
fashions of several countrymen; but my secretary, I think he
hath sufficiently instructed me.   85

BIANCA
How, my lord?

BILIOSO
'Marry, my good lord', quoth he, 'your lordship shall ever
find amongst a hundred Frenchmen, forty hot-shots;
amongst a hundred Spaniards, threescore braggarts;
amongst a hundred Dutchmen, fourscore drunkards;   90
amongst a hundred Englishmen, fourscore and ten
madmen; and amongst an hundred Welshmen – '

BIANCA
What, my lord?

BILIOSO
'Fourscore and nineteen gentlemen'.

BIANCA
But since you go about a sad embassy, I would have you go   95
in black, my lord.

BILIOSO
Why, dost think I cannot mourn unless I wear my hat in
cypress like an alderman's heir? That's vile, very old, in
faith.

74–5 *Scotch boot* a torture instrument in which the ankles were crushed
75 *French harlequin* possibly a reference to a *commedia dell'arte* routine featuring
    a quack doctor or mountebank
84 *several countrymen* different countries
88 *hot-shots* reckless hot-heads
92 *Welshmen* Compare Overbury's character of 'A Welchman': 'He accompts none
    well descended, that call him not Cosen' (ed. Paylor, p. 18).
95 *sad* serious
98 *cypress* transparent black veiling
    old unfashionable

BIANCA

I'll learn of you shortly. Oh, we should have a fine gallant   100
of you should not I instruct you! How will you bear yourself when you come into the Duke of Florence' court?

BILIOSO

Proud enough, and 'twill do well enough. As I walk up and
down the chamber, I'll spit frowns about me, have a strong
perfume in my jerkin, let my beard grow to make me look   105
terrible, salute no man beneath the fourth button, and 'twill
do excellent.

BIANCA

But there is a very beautiful lady there; how will you entertain her?

BILIOSO

I'll tell you that when the lady hath entertained me. But to   110
satisfy thee, here comes the fool.

Enter PASSARELLO

Fool, thou shalt stand for the fair lady.

PASSARELLO

Your fool will stand for your lady most willingly and most
uprightly.

BILIOSO

I'll salute her in Latin.   115

PASSARELLO

Oh, your fool can understand no Latin.

BILIOSO

Ay, but your lady can.

PASSARELLO

Why then, if your lady take down your fool, your fool will
stand no longer for your lady.

BILIOSO

A pestilent fool! 'Fore God, I think the world be turned   120
upside down too.

PASSARELLO

Oh no, sir; for then your lady and all the ladies in the palace
should go with their heels upward, and that were a strange
sight, you know.

BILIOSO

There be many will repine at my preferment.   125

---

106 *salute ... button* not show an extreme degree of respect by bowing lower than
   the middle of the chest
110 *the lady* the Duchess of Florence
113–14 *stand for ... uprightly* a bawdy pun, continued in ll. 118–19
118 *take down* (i) humiliate, put in one's place (ii) bring low

PASARELLO
Oh ay, like the envy of an elder sister that hath her younger
made a lady before her.

BILIOSO
The Duke is wondrous discontented.

PASSARELLO
Ay, and more melancholic than a usurer having all his
money out at the death of a prince.   130

BILIOSO
Didst thou see Madam Floria today?

PASSARELLO
Yes, I found her repairing her face today; the red upon the
white showed as if her cheeks should have been served in
for two dishes of barberries in stewed broth, and the flesh
to them a woodcock.   135

BILIOSO
A bitter fowl! Come, madam, this night thou shalt enjoy me
freely, and tomorrow for Florence.

[BIANCA *and* BILIOSO *withdraw*; BIANCA *exits*]

PASSARELLO
What a natural fool is he that would be a pair of bodies to
a woman's petticoat, to be trussed and pointed to them!
Well, I'll dog my lord, and the word is proper: for when I   140
fawn upon him, he feeds me; when I snap him by the
fingers, he spits in my mouth. If a dog's death were not
strangling, I had rather be one than a serving man; for the
corruption of coin is either the generation of a usurer, or a
lousy beggar.   *Exit* 145

127 *made a lady* marry a titled husband, distressing because the elder must thereafter
     defer socially to the younger
130 *out* lent out
     the death of a prince whose successor might cancel previous debts
133–5 *her cheeks ... woodcock* The coloured make-up over a base of white lead on
     Madame Floria's cheeks is compared to bitter red berries served in the white
     broth of a stewed woodcock.
136 *bitter fowl* with a pun on sharp satirical fooling, like that of the Fool in *King
     Lear* I.iv.135. Some editors modernise the spelling to 'fool', but this obscures the
     reference to the woodock.
138 *a pair of bodies* i.e. a bodice or corset, but here with a pun on 'body'
139 *trussed and pointed* tied and laced, as the corset was to the petticoat
144 *corruption* (i) misuse, perversion (ii) dissolution, loss

[Act III,] Scene ii

Enter MALEVOLE *in some frieze gown, whilst* BILIOSO
reads his patent

MALEVOLE

I cannot sleep; my eyes' ill-neighbouring lids
Will hold no fellowship. Oh thou pale sober night,
Thou that in sluggish fumes all sense dost steep,
Thou that gives all the world full leave to play,
Unbend'st the feebled veins of sweaty labour: 5
The galley-slave, that all the toilsome day
Tugs at his oar against the stubborn wave,
Straining his rugged veins, snores fast;
The stooping scythe-man that doth barb the field
Thou makest wink sure. In night all creatures sleep;   10
Only the malcontent, that 'gainst his fate
Repines and quarrels, alas, he's good-man tell-clock!
His sallow jawbones sink with wasting moan;
Whilst others' beds are down, his pillow's stone.

BILIOSO [*Coming forward*]

Malevole!   15

MALEVOLE

Elder of Israel, thou honest defect of wicked nature and
obstinate ignorance, when did thy wife let thee lie with her?

BILIOSO

I am going ambassador to Florence.

---

0 s.d. 1 *frieze* coarse woollen cloth
         2 *patent* commission as ambassador
2–14 Adapted from Sylvester's translation of Du Bartas, *The Divine Weeks*, where
         it is poets who are sleepless. See Appendix, 3.
2 *sober* (i) quiet, peaceful (ii) subdued in tone, not bright
5 *Unbend'st* Relaxes, frees from occupation
9 *barb* mow
10 *wink* shut one's eyes
12 *tell-clock* one who lies awake counting the chimes
16 *Elder of Israel* Malevole is probably thinking of the elders described in the apoc-
         ryphal book of Susannah, verse 5: 'The same year were appointed two of the
         Ancients to be judges, such as the Lord spoke of, that wickedness came from
         Babylon from ancient judges' (1611 translation).
         honest undisguised, self-evident
         defect of wicked nature Quoted from the description of the satyr in *Il Pastor
         Fido* II.vi (sig. G1).

MALEVOLE

Ambassador! Now, for thy country's honour, prithee do
not put up mutton and porridge i' thy cloak-bag. Thy   20
young lady wife goes to Florence with thee too, does she
not?

BILIOSO

No, I leave her at the palace.

MALEVOLE

At the palace? Now discretion shield man! For God's love,
let's ha' no more cuckolds! Hymen begins to put off his   25
saffron robe; keep thy wife i' the state of grace. Heart o'
truth, I would sooner leave my lady singled in a bordello
than in the Genoa palace:
Sin there appearing in her sluttish shape
Would soon grow loathsome, even to blushless sense;   30
Surfeit would choke intemperate appetite,
Make the soul scent the rotten breath of lust;
When in an Italian lascivious palace,
A lady guardianless,
Left to the push of all allurement,   35
The strongest incitements to immodesty –
To have her bound, incensed with wanton sweets,
Her veins filled high with heating delicates,
Soft rest, sweet music, amorous masquerers,
Lascivious banquets, sin itself gilt-o'er,   40

---

20 *mutton and porridge* Bilioso's customary, but unsophisticated foods
     i' thy Q1–2 (in thy Q3)
24 *discretion shield man* may sound judgement protect mankind from folly. Some
     editors emend to 'discretion shield, man'.
25–6 *Hymen ... robe* i.e. even the god of marriage begins to despair of married
     fidelity and puts aside his priestly robes
27 *singled* alone
     bordello brothel
29 ed. (prose in Qq)
30 *blushless* ed. (blushes Qq)
31 *choke* ed. (cloke Qq). I follow Hunter's and Dodsley's emendations here to
     maintain the contrast between the bordello (the 'there' of 1.29), where too much
     sin would become revolting even to those without shame, and the palace, where
     sin is enticing even to the virtuous.
37 *bound* (i) leap about, dance, or perhaps (ii) subject to, rendered powerless by
38 *heating delicates* delicacies that fire the blood
39–50 ed. (prose in Qq)

Strong fantasy tricking up strange delights,
Presenting it dressed pleasingly to sense,
Sense leading it unto the soul, confirmed
With potent example, impudent custom,
Enticed by that great bawd, Opportunity;   45
Thus being prepared, clap to her easy ear,
Youth in good clothes, well-shapèd, rich,
Fair-spoken, promising-noble, ardent, blood-full,
Witty, flattering – Ulysses absent,
Oh Ithaca, can chastest Penelope hold out?   50

BILIOSO
Mass, I'll think on't. Farewell.

MALEVOLE
Farewell. Take thy wife with thee. Farewell.

Exit BILIOSO

To Florence, um? It may prove good, it may,
And we may once unmask our brows.

[Act III,] Scene iii

Enter Count CELSO

CELSO
My honoured lord.

MALEVOLE
Celso, peace, how is't? Speak low; pale fears
Suspect that hedges, walls, and trees have ears.
Speak, how runs all?

CELSO
I' faith, my lord, that beast with many heads,   5
The staggering multitude, recoils apace:

41–5 The process of temptation described here is opposite to the normative ideal of Elizabethan moral psychology in which all sensory impressions and fantasies should be referred immediately to the rational soul for judgement. See *The Scourge of Villainie* VIII.173–210 and Davenport's notes.

41 *tricking up* adorning artfully

45 *that great bawd, Opportunity* From Shakespeare, *The Rape of Lucrece*, ll. 876, 886.

50 *Ithaca, can* Q1–2 (Ithacan Q3)

can ... out? Compare Ovid, *Ars Amatoria* I.477, where Ovid promises that the persistent suitor will overcome Penelope herself.

2–4 cd. (prose in Qq)

5 *beast ... heads* Though Marston condemns tyrannical abuses, like most

Though thorough great men's envy, most men's malice,
Their much intemperate heat hath banished you,
Yet now they find envy and malice ne'er
Produce faint reformation.   10
The Duke, the too-soft Duke, lies as a block
For which two tugging factions seem to saw,
But still the iron through the ribs they draw.

MALEVOLE
I tell thee, Celso, I have ever found
Thy breast most far from shifting cowardice   15
And fearful baseness. Therefore, I'll tell thee, Celso,
I find the wind begins to come about;
I'll shift my suit of fortune.
I know the Florentine, whose only force,
By marrying his proud daughter to this prince,   20
Both banished me and made this weak lord Duke,
Will now forsake them all; be sure he will.
I'll lie in ambush for conveniency,
Upon their severance to confirm myself.

CELSO
Is Ferneze interred?   25

MALEVOLE
Of that at leisure; he lives.

CELSO
But how stands Mendoza? How is't with him?

MALEVOLE
Faith, like a pair of snuffers: snibs filth in other men and
retains it in himself.

CELSO
He does fly from public notice, methinks, as a hare does   30
from hounds: the feet whereon he flies betrays him.

MALEVOLE
I can track him, Celso.

Elizabethan writers and their Roman models he is contemptuous of popular
opinion. His metaphor here is from Horace, *Epistles*, I.i.76.

9-10 *they ... reformation* the multitude finds that the nobles' envy and the
majority's malice does not produce even a faint reformation

18-19 ed. (Ile ... force,/ Qq)

19 *only force* force alone

24 *Upon ... myself* i.e. to reclaim his dukedom when Florence abandons Pietro

28 *snuffers* candle-snuffers

snibs (i) trims off, as a dirty wick (ii) reproves

29 *himself* Q1-2 (itself Q3)

Oh, my disguise fools him most powerfully.
For that I seem a desperate malcontent,
He fain would clasp with me; he is the true slave   35
That will put on the most affected grace
For some vile second cause.

Enter MENDOZA

CELSO   He's here.
MALEVOLE   Give place.

                                        CELSO [*retires*]

Illo, ho, ho, ho! Art there, old true-penny? Where hast thou
spent thyself this morning? I see flattery in thine eyes and
damnation i' thy soul. Ha, ye huge rascal!   40
MENDOZA
Thou art very merry.
MALEVOLE
As a scholar *futuens gratis*. How does the Devil go with
thee, now?
MENDOZA
Malevole, thou art an arrant knave.
MALEVOLE
Who I? I have been a sergeant, man.   45
MENDOZA
Thou art very poor.
MALEVOLE
As Job, an alchemist, or a poet.
MENDOZA
The Duke hates thee.

35 *clasp* ally himself
36-7 *put on ... cause* as Mendoza pretends friendship to employ Malevole in vil-
     lainy
37 *second cause* ulterior motive
38 *Illo ... true-penny?* This echo of *Hamlet* I.v.116 and 150 both fits Malevole's
   zany persona and mocks Mendoza as a false comrade.
40 *i' thy* Q1–2 (in thy Q3)
   ye Q1–2 (thou Q3)
42 *futuens gratis* having sex for free
   does Q1–2 (doth Q3)
45 *sergeant* an officer who made arrests
47 *alchemist* An ironic joke, since alchemists claimed to be able to turn base metal
   into gold.

MALEVOLE

As Irishmen do bum-cracks.

MENDOZA

Thou hast lost his amity.   50

MALEVOLE

As pleasing as maids lose their virginity.

MENDOZA

Would thou wert of a lusty spirit! Would thou wert noble!

MALEVOLE

Why, sure my blood gives me I am noble; sure I am of noble
kind, for I find myself possessed with all their qualities: love
dogs, dice, and drabs; scorn wit in stuff-clothes; have beat   55
my shoemaker, knocked my seamstress, cuckold' my
'pothecary, and undone my tailor. Noble, why not? Since
the Stoic said, *Neminem servum non ex regibus, neminem
regem non ex servis esse oriundum*; only busy Fortune
touses, and the provident chances blends them together. I'll   60
give you a simile: did you e'er see a well with two buckets,
whilst one comes up full to be emptied, another goes down
empty to be filled? Such is the state of all humanity. Why,
look you, I may be the son of some duke; for, believe me,
intemperate lascivious bastardy makes nobility doubtful. I   65
have a lusty, daring heart, Mendoza.

MENDOZA

Let's grasp; I do like thee infinitely. Wilt enact one thing for
me?

MALEVOLE

Shall I get by it? ([MENDOZA] *gives him his purse*)
Command me; I am thy slave, beyond death and hell.   70

MENDOZA

Murder the Duke!

MALEVOLE

My heart's wish, my soul's desire, my fantasy's dream,
My blood's longing, the only height of my hopes!

---

49 *As ... bum-cracks* Compare Nashe, *Works* (ed. McKerrow) I.188: 'The Irishman
    will draw his dagger and be ready to kill and slay, if one break wind in his
    company'.

55 *scorn ... stuff-clothes* act haughtily toward scholars wearing coarsely woven
    clothes

58–9 *Neminem ... oriundum* Seneca, *Moral Epistles* XLIV.4, quoting Plato: 'There
    is no slave not derived from kings, no king not descended from slaves'.

60 *touses* pulls about roughly, disorders

67 *grasp* embrace

73–5 ed. (My ... How?/Oh God ... together,/ Qq). In his mock enthusiasm,
    Malevole's speech rises to blank verse of irregular length.

How, oh God, how?
Oh how my united spirits throng together!   75
So strengthen my resolve!

MENDOZA
The Duke is now a-hunting.

MALEVOLE
Excellent, admirable, as the Devil would have it! Lend me
– lend me rapier, pistol, crossbow; so, so, I'll do it.

MENDOZA
Then we agree?   80

MALEVOLE
As Lent and fishmongers! Come, *a-cap-a-pie*, how in form?

MENDOZA
Know that this weak-brained Duke, who only stands
On Florence' stilts, hath out of witless zeal
Made me his heir and secretly confirmed
The wreath to me after his life's full point.   85

MALEVOLE
Upon what merit?

MENDOZA
Merit! By heaven, I horn him;
Only Ferneze's death gave me state's life.
Tut, we are politic; he must not live now.

MALEVOLE
No reason, marry. But how must he die now?   90

MENDOZA
My utmost project is to murder the Duke, that I might have
his state, because he makes me his heir; to banish the
Duchess, that I might be rid of a cunning Lacedaemonian,
because I know Florence will forsake her; and then to
marry Maria, the banished Duke Altofront's wife, that her   95
friends might strengthen me and my faction – this is all, la.

---

76 *So* Qq. Some editors emend to 'to'.

81 *Lent* when eating meat was forbidden
   Come, a-cap-a-pie ed. (Come *a cape a pe* Qq) *a-cap-a-pie* Fr., 'from head to
   foot', i.e. from beginning to end. Hunter suggests that Malevole is asking
   whether Pietro comes armed from head to toe, but Mendoza never speaks to that
   question.
   how in form? Qq. Some editors read 'How? Inform'.

82–5 ed. (prose in Qq)

85 *wreath* crown
   full point end

87–9 ed. (prose in Qq)

88 *gave . . . life* kept my political plot alive

93 *Lacedaemonian* slang for 'whore'

MALEVOLE

Do you love Maria?

MENDOZA

Faith, no great affection, but as wise men do love great
women, to ennoble their blood and augment their revenue.
To accomplish this now, thus now: the Duke is in the forest   100
next the sea; single him, kill him, hurl him i' the main, and
proclaim thou sawest wolves eat him.

MALEVOLE

Um, not so good. Methinks when he is slain, to get some
hypocrite, some dangerous wretch that's muffled o'er with
feigned holiness to swear he heard the Duke on some steep   105
cliff lament his wife's dishonour, and, in an agony of his
heart's torture, hurled his groaning sides into the swollen
sea. This circumstance, well-made, sounds probable; and
hereupon the Duchess –

MENDOZA

May well be banished.   110
Oh unpeerable invention! Rare!
Thou god of policy, it honeys me!

MALEVOLE

Then fear not for the wife of Altofront; I'll close to her.

MENDOZA

Thou shalt, thou shalt; our excellency is pleased.
Why wert not thou an emperor? When we   115
Are Duke, I'll make thee some great man, sure.

MALEVOLE

Nay, make me some rich knave, and I'll make myself some
great man.

MENDOZA

In thee be all my spirit: retain ten souls,
Unite thy virtual powers, resolve;   120
Ha, remember greatness! Heart, farewell.
The fate of all my hopes in thee doth dwell.   [*Exit*]

CELSO [*comes forward*]

---

101 *i' the* Q1–2 (in the Q3)
104 *muffled o'er* ed. (muffled, or Qq)
108 *circumstance* tale, long narrative
110–12 ed. (prose in Qq)
111 *unpeerable* peerless
113 *close to* come to terms with
114–16 ed. (prose in Qq)
119–22 ed. (prose in Qq)
120 *virtual* effective

MALEVOLE
  Celso, didst hear? Oh Heaven, didst hear
  Such devilish mischief? Sufferest thou the world
  Carouse damnation even with greedy swallow,   125
  And still dost wink, still does thy vengeance slumber?
  If now thy brows are clear, when will they thunder?

                                    [*Exeunt*]

[Act III,] Scene iv

Enter PIETRO, FERRARDO, PREPASSO, *and three* PAGES.
Cornets like horns

FERRARDO
  The dogs are at a fault.
PIETRO
  Would God nothing but the dogs were at it! Let the deer
  pursue safety, the dogs follow the game, and do you follow
  the dogs. As for me, 'tis unfit one beast should hunt
  another; I ha' one chaseth me. And't please you, I would be   5
  rid of ye a little.
FERRARDO
  Would your grief would as soon leave you as we to quiet-
  ness.
PIETRO
  I thank you.

               Exeunt [FERRARDO *and* PREPASSO]

  Boy, what dost thou dream of now?   10
PAGE
  Of a dry summer, my lord, for here's a hot world towards;
  but my lord, I had a strange dream last night.

123–7 Paraphrased from Seneca, *Phaedra* 671–74, where Hippolytus is outraged at
    Phaedra's lustful advances.
125 *Carouse* Drink down without stopping
126 *wink* turn a blind eye
127 *clear* smooth, untroubled

  1 *at a fault* hunting term for losing the scent; Pietro's reply puns on the meaning
     'moral defect', indicating his preoccupation with Aurelia's adultery
  3 *safety* ed. (safely Qq)
  4–5 *one ... another* i.e. his cuckold's horns make Pietro, the hunter, a beast as well
  6 *ye* Q1–2 (you Q3)
  7 *would ... we* Q3 (would, as soon as we, leave you Q1–2)
  11 *towards* coming on

PIETRO

What strange dream?

PAGE

Why, methought I pleased you with singing, and then I
dreamt you gave me that short sword.   15

PIETRO

Prettily begged! Hold thee, I'll prove thy dream true; tak't.

[*Gives sword*]

PAGE [*Kneeling*]

My duty. But still I dreamt on, my lord, and methought,
and't shall please your excellency, you would needs out of
your royal bounty give me that jewel in your hat.

PIETRO

Oh, thou didst but dream, boy; do not believe it. Dreams   20
prove not always true: they may hold in a short sword, but
not in a jewel. But now, sir, you dreamt you had pleased me
with singing; make that true as I ha' made the other.

PAGE

Faith, my lord, I did but dream, and dreams, you say, prove
not always true: they may hold in a good sword, but not in   25
a good song. The truth is, I ha' lost my voice.

PIETRO

Lost thy voice! How?

PAGE

With dreaming, faith; but here's a couple of sirenical rascals
shall enchant ye. What shall they sing, my good lord?

PIETRO

Sing of the nature of women, and then the song shall be   30
surely full of variety, old crotchets, and most sweet closes;
it shall be humorous, grave, fantastic, amorous, melancholy, sprightly – one in all, and all in one.

PAGE

All in one?

PIETRO

By 'r lady, too many. Sing; my speech grows culpable of   35
unthrifty idleness; sing.

The song

23 *ha'* Q1–2 (have Q3)
31 *crotchets* (i) quarter-notes (ii) whimsical fancies
    closes conclusions to its musical phrases
34 *one* (i) one song (ii) one woman, i.e. Aurelia, either as a woman of inconstant
    moods or multiple lovers. Pietro's response indicates that he takes it in the latter
    sense.

Ah, so, so, sing. I am heavy; walk off; I shall talk in my
sleep; walk off.

Exeunt PAGES. [PIETRO *sleeps*]

[Act III,] Scene v

Enter MALEVOLE, *with crossbow and pistol*

MALEVOLE
Brief, brief, who? The Duke? Good heaven, that fools
should stumble upon greatness! – Do not sleep, Duke; give
ye good morrow. Must be brief, Duke; I am feed to murder
thee. Start not! Mendoza, Mendoza hired me; here's his
gold, his pistol, crossbow, sword; 'tis all as firm as earth.   5
Oh fool, fool, choked with the common maze of easy idiots,
credulity! Make him thine heir! What, thy sworn murderer!
PIETRO
Oh, can it be?
MALEVOLE
Can!
PIETRO
Discovered he not Ferneze?   10
MALEVOLE
Yes, but why? But why? For love to thee? Much, much! To
be revenged upon his rival, who had thrust his jaws awry;
who being slain, supposed by thine own hands, defended by
his sword, made thee most loathsome, him most gracious
with thy loose princess. Thou, closely yielding egress and   15
regress to her, madest him heir, whose hot unquiet lust
straight toused thy sheets, and now would seize thy state.
Politician! Wise man! Death, to be led to the stake like a
bull by the horns, to make even kindness cut a gentle
throat! Life, why art thou numbed? Thou foggy dullness,   20
speak! Lives not more faith in a home-thrusting tongue,
than in these fencing tip-tap courtiers?

Enter CELSO *with a hermit's gown and beard*

37–8 ed. (placed at the beginning of III.v in Qq)

 3 *Must* Q1–2 (You must Q3)
    feed paid
 5 *sword* Q1–2 (and sword Q3)
 6 *maze* delusion
    easy idiots credulous simpletons
17 *toused thy sheets* rumpled your bed, i.e. slept with your wife
21–2 *home-thrusting ... courtiers* The contrast is between the blunt critic who

PIETRO
  Lord, Malevole, if this be true –
MALEVOLE
  If! Come, shade thee with this disguise. If! Thou shalt
  handle it; he shall thank thee for killing thyself. Come,   25
  follow my directions, and thou shalt see strange sleights.
PIETRO
  World, whither wilt thou?
MALEVOLE
  Why, to the Devil. Come, the morn grows late;
  A steady quickness is the soul of state.

                                                    Exeunt

Act IV, Scene i

            Enter MAQUERELLE *knocking at the ladies' door*

MAQUERELLE
  Medam, medam, are you stirring, medam? If you be stirring, medam – if I thought I should disturb ye –

                        [*Enter* PAGE]

PAGE
  My lady is up, forsooth.
MAQUERELLE
  A pretty boy, faith, how old art thou?
PAGE
  I think fourteen.   5
MAQUERELLE
  Nay, and ye be in the teens, are ye a gentleman born? Do
  you know me? My name is Medam Maquerelle; I lie in the
  old Cunny Court.

                    Enter BIANCA *and* EMILIA

----

  fights straightforwardly in the old English fashion and the flattering courtier
  whose verbal feints are like the newly elaborate style of Italian fencing satirised
  in *Romeo and Juliet* II.iv.20–4.
23 s.p. PIETRO ed. (Celso Qq)
   Lord, Malevole ed. (Lord Malevole Qq)
29 *state* statecraft

 1 *Medam* an affected pronunciation
 6 *and ... teens* i.e. if you are above the age of consent
 8 *Cunny Court* Rabbit Yard, an appropriate locale for a bawd, given the customary pun on 'Cunny'

See here the ladies.

BIANCA
A fair day to ye, Maquerelle.   10

EMILIA
Is the Duchess up yet, sentinel?

MAQUERELLE
Oh ladies, the most abominable mischance! Oh dear ladies,
the most piteous disaster! Ferneze was taken last night in
the Duchess' chamber. Alas, the Duke catched him and
killed him!   15

BIANCA
Was he found in bed?

MAQUERELLE
Oh no, but the villainous certainty is, the door was not
bolted, the tongue-tied hatch held his peace; so, the naked
truth is, he was found in his shirt, whilst I, like an arrant
beast, lay in the outward chamber, heard nothing; and yet   20
they came by me in the dark, and yet I felt them not, like a
senseless creature as I was. Oh beauties, look to your busk-
points, if not chastely, yet charily: be sure the door be
bolted. – Is your lord gone to Florence?

BIANCA
Yes, Maquerelle.   25

MAQUERELLE
I hope you'll find the discretion to purchase a fresh gown
'fore his return. – Now, by my troth, beauties, I would ha'
ye once wise: he loves ye, pish! He is witty, bubble! Fair-
proportioned, mew! Nobly-born, wind! Let this be still
your fixed position: esteem me every man according to his   30
good gifts, and so ye shall ever remain 'most dear, and most
worthy to be most dear' ladies.

EMILIA
Is the Duke returned from hunting yet?

---

18   *tongue-tied hatch* i.e. the oiled hinges of the half-door
19   *in his shirt* only in his shirt, the customary nightdress
22   *senseless* unconscious
22–3 *busk-points* laces that fastened the whalebone stays, here used as a metaphor
      for 'defences' in general
27   *'fore* Q1–2 (for Q3) before, so that he cannot overrule her purchase
31   *good gifts* not the good qualities enumerated above, but rich presents
31–2 *'most ... most dear'* An ironic quotation from Sidney's dedication of *The
      Arcadia* to the Countess of Pembroke.

MAQUERELLE
They say not yet.
BIANCA
'Tis now in midst of day.   35
EMILIA
How bears the Duchess with this blemish now?
MAQUERELLE
Faith, boldly; strongly defies defame, as one that has a duke
to her father. And there's a note to you: be sure of a stout
friend in a corner, that may always awe your husband.
Mark the 'haviour of the Duchess now: she dares defame,   40
cries 'Duke, do what thou canst, I'll 'quite mine honour';
nay, as one confirmed in her own virtue against ten thousand mouths that mutter her disgrace, she's presently for
dances.

                    Enter FERRARDO

BIANCA
For dances!   45
MAQUERELLE
Most true.
EMILIA
Most strange. See, here's my servant, young Ferrard. How
many servants think'st thou I have, Maquerelle?
MAQUERELLE
The more, the merrier. 'Twas well said, 'use your servants
as you do your smocks': have many, use one, and change   50
often, for that's most sweet and court-like.
FERRARDO
Save ye, fair ladies, is the Duke returned?
BIANCA
Sweet sir, no voice of him as yet in court.
FERRARDO
'Tis very strange.
BIANCA
And how like you my servant, Maquerelle?   55

39 *friend* relative
40 *dares defame* defies disgrace
41 *'quite* ed. (quite Qq) requite, avenge. Some editors read as 'quit' for 'acquit'
43 *presently* immediately
47 *my servant* Some editors assign this speech to Bianca in light of l. 55 and
    Ferrardo's courtship of Bianca in V.vi, but perhaps he is involved with both
    women.
49–51 From *Il Pastor Fido* I.iii (sig. C3v) and attributed by Corisca to a city lady
    who taught her the art of love.

MAQUERELLE

I think he could hardly draw Ulysses' bow, but by my
fidelity, were his nose narrower, his eyes broader, his hands
thinner, his lips thicker, his legs bigger, his feet lesser, his
hair blacker, and his teeth whiter, he were a tolerable sweet
youth, i' faith. And he will come to my chamber, I will read   60
him the fortune of his beard.

Cornets sound

FERRARDO

Not yet returned I fear – but the Duchess approacheth.

[Act IV,] Scene ii

Enter MENDOZA *supporting the Duchess* [AURELIA],
GUERRINO. *The ladies that are on the stage rise.*
FERRARDO *ushers in the Duchess and then takes a lady
to tread a measure*

AURELIA

We will dance – music! – We will dance.

GUERRINO

'Les quanto', lady, 'Pensez bien', 'Passa regis', or 'Bianca's
brawl'?

AURELIA

We have forgot the brawl.

FERRARDO

So soon? 'Tis wonder.   5

GUERRINO

Why, 'tis but two singles on the left, two on the right, three
doubles forward, a traverse of six round; do this twice,
three singles side, galliard trick of twenty, coranto-pace; a

---

56 *draw ... bow* Penelope's test of her suitors' worthiness to claim her hand. See
   The Odyssey XXI.

62 *Not ... approacheth* ed. (Not yet returnd I feare, but/The Dutches approcheth/
   Qq). Some editors place a question mark after 'returned'.

2–3 '*Les quanto ... brawl*' apparently the names of contemporary dances. '*Les
   quanto*' may be the 'courtlie daunce, called *Les Guanto*' mentioned in Antony
   Munday's *Banquet of Daintie Conceits* (1588). The second and the third, 'The
   King's Dance', are unknown. The 'brawl' or 'branle' was a dance in duple time
   in which the dancers primarily moved sideways.

6–10 'Singles' and 'doubles' are dance steps of varying complexity. The 'trick of
   twenty' is probably a caper or high kick like those in the galliard, a lively dance
   in triple time, consisting of five movements of the feet and ending in a 'sault' or

figure of eight, three singles broken down, come up, meet,
two doubles, fall back, and then honour.   10

AURELIA
Oh Daedalus, thy maze! I have quite forgot it.

MAQUERELLE
Trust me, so have I, saving the falling back and then
honour.

Enter PREPASSO. [*Music ceases*]

AURELIA
Music, music!

PREPASSO
Who saw the Duke? The Duke?   15

Enter EQUATO

AURELIA
Music!

EQUATO
The Duke? Is the Duke returned?

AURELIA
Music!

Enter CELSO

CELSO
The Duke is either quite invisible, or else is not.

AURELIA
We are not pleased with your intrusion upon our private   20
retirement. We are not pleased. You have forgot yourselves.

Enter a PAGE

CELSO
Boy, thy master? Where's the Duke?

PAGE
Alas, I left him burying the earth with his spread joyless

---

leap, here performed at the fast pace of the coranto, or 'running dance'. For
descriptions of contemporary dances, see Thoinot Arbeau (Jehan Tabouret),
Orchesography, trans. Mary Stewart Evans, with an introduction by Julia Sutton
(1967).

9 *broken down* divided into shorter, quicker steps

10 *fall back ... honour* step back and then curtsy

12 *saving* except for. Maquerelle finds 'falling back' (in the bawdy sense) easy to
remember.

17 s.p. *EQUATO* Q1 (not in Q2; PREPASSO Q3)

23 *burying* covering

limbs. He told me he was heavy, would sleep; bade me walk
off for that the strength of fantasy oft made him talk in his   25
dreams. I straight obeyed, nor ever saw him since; but,
wheresoe'er he is, he's sad.

AURELIA
Music, sound high, as is our heart, sound high!

[*Music plays*]

[Act IV,] Scene iii

Enter MALEVOLE *and* PIETRO *disguised like a hermit*

MALEVOLE
The Duke – peace! [*Music ceases*] – The Duke is dead.
AURELIA
  Music!
MALEVOLE
  Is't music?
MENDOZA
  Give proof.
FERRARDO
  How?   5
CELSO
  Where?
PREPASSO
  When?
MALEVOLE
Rest in peace as the Duke does; quietly sit. For my own part
I beheld him but dead, that's all. Marry, here's one can give
you a more particular account of him.   10
MENDOZA
Speak, holy father, nor let any brow
Within this presence fright thee from the truth.
Speak confidently and freely.
AURELIA   We attend.
PIETRO
Now had the mounting sun's all-ripening wings
Swept the cold sweat of night from earth's dank breast,   15
When I (whom men call Hermit of the Rock)

---

24 *bade* Q1–2 (bid Q3)

11–13 ed. (prose in Qq)

14–45 Of the many possible analogues, Pietro's description seems particularly
    indebted to Ariosto's description of Ariodant's supposed suicide in *Orlando
    Furioso*, Bk. V, stanzas 53–9, and Tasso's description of his hero's attempted

Forsook my cell and clambered up a cliff,
Against whose base the heady Neptune dashed
His high-curled brows. There 'twas I eased my limbs,
When, lo, my entrails melted with the moan   20
Some one, who far 'bove me was climbed, did make –
I shall offend –

MENDOZA
  Not.

AURELIA
  On.

PIETRO
  Methinks I hear him yet: 'Oh female faith!   25
  Go sow the ingrateful sand and love a woman!
  And do I live to be the scoff of men?
  To be the wittol cuckold, even to hug
  My poison? Thou knowest, oh truth!
  Sooner hard steel will melt with southern wind,   30
  A seaman's whistle calm the ocean,
  A town on fire be extinct with tears,
  Than women, vowed to blushless impudence,
  With sweet behaviour and soft minioning,
  Will turn from that where appetite is fixed.   35
  Oh powerful blood, how thou dost slave their soul!
  I washed an Ethiope, who for recompence
  Sullied my name. And must I then be forced
  To walk, to live thus black? Must? Must? – Fie!
  He that can bear with "must", he cannot die.'   40
  With that he sighed so passionately deep
  That the dull air even groaned; at last he cries,
  'Sink shame in seas, sink deep enough!': so dies.
  For then I viewed his body fall and souse
  Into the foamy main; oh then I saw   45
  That which methinks I see: it was the Duke,

---

suicide in *Aminta*, IV.ii and V.i, though the latter is not motivated by belief in
his beloved's infidelity, as Ariodant's is. Harris points out the general parallel
with the false report of Orestes' death by the disguised Pylades and Orestes.

18 *heady* violent, headstrong
    Neptune the sea god
28 *the* Q3 (their Q1–2)
32 *extinct* extinguished
34 *minioning* caressing
36 *blood* sexual passion
41 *so* Q1 (too Q2–3)
44 *souse* plunge

Whom straight the nicer-stomached sea belched up.
But then –
MALEVOLE
Then came I in, but 'las, all was too late,
For even straight he sunk.   50
PIETRO
Such was the Duke's sad fate.
CELSO
A better fortune to our Duke Mendoza!
ALL
Mendoza!

Cornets flourish

MENDOZA
A guard, a guard!

Enter a guard

We, full of hearty tears
For our good father's loss –   55
For so we well may call him
Who did beseech your loves for our succession –
Cannot so lightly over-jump his death
As leave his woes revengeless. (*To* AURELIA) Woman of
    shame,
We banish thee for ever to the place   60
From whence this good man comes, nor permit on death
Unto the body any ornament;
But, base as was thy life, depart away.
AURELIA
Ungrateful!
MENDOZA
Away!   65
AURELIA
Villain, hear me!

PREPASSO *and* GUERRINO *lead away the Duchess* [AURELIA]

47–8 ed. (Whom ... sea/Belcht ... then/ Qq)
47 *nicer-stomached* fastidious in appetite
    belched Compare Shakespeare, *The Tempest* III.iii.53–6: 'You are three men of
    sin, whom Destiny, / ... the never surfeited sea / Hath caus'd to belch up you'.
53 s.p. *ALL* ed. (OMNES Q2–3; Cry all Q1)
54 *hearty* heartfelt
61–2 ed. (From ... comes/Nor ... ornament/ Qq)

MENDOZA
  Be gone! My lords,
  Address to public council; 'tis most fit,
  The train of Fortune is borne up by wit.
  Away; our presence shall be sudden; haste.   70

          All depart saving MENDOZA, MALEVOLE, *and* PIETRO

MALEVOLE
  Now, you egregious devil! Ha, ye murdering politician!
  How dost, Duke? How dost look now? Brave Duke, i'
  faith!
MENDOZA
  How did you kill him?
MALEVOLE
  Slatted his brains out, then soused him in the briny sea.   75
MENDOZA
  Brained him and drowned him too?
MALEVOLE
  Oh 'twas best, sure work: *for he that strikes a great man,*
  let him strike home, or else 'ware, he'll prove no man;
  shoulder not a huge fellow unless you may be sure to lay
  him in the kennel.   80
MENDOZA
  A most sound brain-pan! I'll make you both emperors.
MALEVOLE
  Make us Christians, make us Christians!
MENDOZA
  I'll hoist ye; ye shall mount.
MALEVOLE
  To the gallows, say ye? Come: *praemium incertum petit*
  certum scelus. How stands the progress?   85
MENDOZA
  Here, take my ring unto the citadel;

67–8 ed. (Be gone ... counsell/'Tis most fit/ Qq
68 *Address to* Prepare for
69 Probably not, as Hunter, Jackson and Neill suggest, a declaration of
   Machiavellian principles, but the pretence of a seemingly legitimate statesman
   who calls for reasoned deliberation to support his accession to power.
75 *slatted* dashed
   soused ... briny i.e. as if he were a dead fish pickled in brine
78 *'ware* beware
80 *kennel* gutter
84–5 *praemium ... scelus* 'he seeks uncertain reward, certain crime', adapted from
   Seneca, *Phoenissae*, 632
86 *take ... citadel* as a sign that Mendoza has really sent him

Have entrance to Maria, the grave Duchess
Of banished Altofront. Tell her we love her;
Omit no circumstance to grace our person. Do't.

MALEVOLE

I'll make an excellent pander. Duke, farewell; 'dieu, adieu,   90
Duke.

MENDOZA

Take Maquerelle with thee, for 'tis found,
None cuts a diamond but a diamond.

                                        Exit MALEVOLE

Hermit, thou art a man for me, my confessor.
O thou selected spirit, born for my good,   95
Sure thou wouldst make an excellent elder
In a deformed church. Come,
We must be inward, thou and I all one.

PIETRO

I am glad I was ordained for ye.

MENDOZA

Go to, then, thou must know that Malevole is a strange vil-   100
lain – dangerous, very dangerous. You see how broad 'a
speaks, a gross-jawed rogue. I would have thee poison him:
he's like a corn upon my great toe, I cannot go for him; he
must be cored out, he must. Wilt do't, ha?

PIETRO

Anything, anything.   105

MENDOZA

Heart of my life, thus then to the citadel:
Thou shalt consort with this Malevole;
There, being at supper, poison him.
It shall be laid upon Maria, who yields love or dies.
Scud quick, like lightning!

PIETRO   *Good deeds crawl, but mischief flies.* 110
                                                        Exit

90 *'dieu, adieu* ed. (due, adue Qq). The original spelling suggests a pun.

96–8 ed. (Sure ... church/Come ... one/ Qq)

96–7 *an ... church* 'Reformed' groups like Presbyterians were ruled by elders. Since
    Mendoza immediately asks the Hermit to poison Malevole, perhaps his use of
    'deformed' reflects his suspicion that deviation from traditional theology goes
    hand in hand with deviation from morality.

98 *inward* intimate

103 *go for* walk because of

110 *Scud ... lightning/Good ... flies* Q3 (Scud quick/Like lightning good ... flies/
    Q1–2). Q1 assigns the second half-line to Pietro; Q2, to Mendoza; Hunter fol-
    lows Q1, but puts a period after 'lightning'.

Enter MALEVOLE

MALEVOLE
Your devilship's ring has no virtue. The buff-captain, the
sallow Westphalian gammon-faced zaza cries, 'Stand out,
must have a stiffer warrant, or no pass into the Castle of
Comfort'.

MENDOZA
Command our sudden letter. Not enter? Shalt – what place   115
is there in Genoa, but thou shalt? – into my heart, into my
very heart. Come, let's love; we must love, we two, soul and
body.

MALEVOLE
How didst like the hermit? A strange hermit, sirrah.

MENDOZA
A dangerous fellow, very perilous. He must die.   120

MALEVOLE
Ay, he must die.

MENDOZA
Thou'st kill him. We are wise; we must be wise.

MALEVOLE
And provident.

MENDOZA
Yea, provident. Beware an hypocrite;
A churchman once corrupted, oh avoid!   125
A fellow that makes religion his stalking-horse,
He breeds a plague. Thou shalt poison him.

MALEVOLE
Ho, 'tis wondrous necessary. How?

---

111 *buff-captain* officer in a leather jerkin
112 *sallow Westphalian gammon-faced* with yellow (i.e. sun-burnt) skin like
    Westphalian bacon
    zaza a nonce-word of uncertain meaning, 'possibly related to "huszar" (Hung.),
    military freebooter' (Harris)
113–14 *Castle of Comfort* Hunter notes that the citadel where Maria is imprisoned
    'is compared to some Court of Love allegory' and that the term may also be slang
    for the *mons veneris*.
115 *Shalt* ed. (shat Qq). Some editors read 'sha't' for 'shalt not'.
122 *Thou'st* Thou must
125 *avoid* Q1–2 (assoid Q3)
126 *stalking-horse* a trained horse or dummy used by hunters to get close to game;
    Q2–3 add a marginal note, '(shoots under his belly)', to explain the term; it is
    sometimes taken as a stage-direction for Mendoza's miming or even as part of
    the dialogue.
127 *Thou … him* ed. (italicised in Qq)

MENDOZA
You both go jointly to the citadel,
There sup, there poison him; and Maria,   130
Because she is our opposite, shall bear
The sad suspect, on which she dies or loves us.

MALEVOLE
I run.   *Exit*

MENDOZA
We that are great, our sole self-good still moves us.
They shall die both, for their deserts craves more   135
Than we can recompense; their presence still
Imbraids our fortunes with beholdingness,
Which we abhor; like deed, not doer. Then conclude,
They live not to cry out 'ingratitude!'.
One stick burns t'other, steel cuts steel alone;   140
'Tis good trust few, but oh, 'tis best trust none.   *Exit*

[Act IV,] Scene iv

Enter MALEVOLE *and* PIETRO, *still disguised, at several doors*

MALEVOLE
How do you? How dost, Duke?

PIETRO
Oh let the last day fall, drop, drop on our cursed heads! Let
heaven unclasp itself, vomit forth flames!

MALEVOLE
Oh do not rand, do not turn player; there's more of them

131 *opposite* opponent
132 *sad suspect* grave suspicion
    on which she dies on account of which she must die
135–9 A common sentiment in 'politic' thinkers. Hunter cites Machiavelli, *The
    Prince*, Chapter III: 'whoever is the cause of another becoming powerful, is
    ruined himself; for that power is produced by him either through craft or force;
    and both of these are suspected by the one who has been raised to power'
    (Modern Library ed., p. 14). Compare also *1 Henry IV* I.iii.285–8.
137 *Imbraids* Upbraids
138 *like deed, not doer* Compare Tilley, K 64: 'A king loves the treason but hates the
    traitor'.

  2 *the last day* the Day of Judgement – another echo of Seneca's *Phaedra*, ll. 680–1
    drop on Q3 (drop in Q1–2)
  4 *rand* rant

than can well live one by another already. What, art an   5
infidel still?

PIETRO

I am amazed, struck in a swoon with wonder! I am commanded to poison thee.

MALEVOLE

I am commanded to poison thee at supper.

PIETRO

At supper?   10

MALEVOLE

In the citadel.

PIETRO

In the citadel?

MALEVOLE

Cross capers, tricks! Truth o' heaven, he would discharge
us as boys do eldern guns, one pellet to strike out another.
Of what faith art now?   15

PIETRO

All is damnation, wickedness extreme; there is no faith in
man.

MALEVOLE

In none but usurers and brokers, they deceive no man; men
take 'em for blood-suckers, and so they are. Now, God
deliver me from my friends.   20

PIETRO

Thy friends?

MALEVOLE

Yes, from my friends, for from mine enemies I'll deliver
myself. Oh, cut-throat friendship is the rankest villainy!
Mark this Mendoza, mark him for a villain; but Heaven
will send a plague upon him for a rogue.   25

PIETRO

Oh world!

MALEVOLE

World! 'Tis the only region of death, the greatest shop of
the Devil, the cruelest prison of men, out of the which none

5–6   an infidel i.e. a disbeliever in Pietro's villainy
13   Cross ... tricks Fancy dance steps. Malevole is amazed at Mendoza's agile plot-
     ting.
14   eldern guns pop-guns made of elder wood
18   s.p. MALEVOLE ed. (MENDOZA Qq)
     brokers pawnbrokers
27–31   In the de contemptu mundi tradition, but possibly influenced by Florio, First
        Fruites: 'O filthy worlde, thou knowest wel that I know thy proceedings, howe
        thou art a grave for the dead, a prison for the quicke, a shop of vices' (fol. 80).

pass without paying their dearest breath for a fee; there's
nothing perfect in it but extreme, extreme calamity, such as   30
comes yonder.

[Act IV,] Scene v

Enter AURELIA, *two Halberds before and two after,*
supported by CELSO *and* FERRARDO; AURELIA *in base*
mourning attire

AURELIA
To banishment, led on to banishment!
PIETRO
Lady, the blessedness of repentance to you.
AURELIA
Why? Why? I can desire nothing
But death, nor deserve anything but hell.
If Heaven should give sufficiency of grace   5
To clear my soul, it would make Heaven graceless;
My sins would make the stock of mercy poor:
Oh, they would try Heaven's goodness to reclaim them.
Judgement is just yet from that vast villain;
But sure he shall not miss sad punishment   10
'Fore he shall rule. On to my cell of shame!
PIETRO
My cell 'tis, lady, where, instead of masques,
Music, tilts, tourneys, and such courtlike shows,
The hollow murmur of the checkless winds
Shall groan again, whilst the unquiet sea   15
Shakes the whole rock with foamy battery;
There usherless the air comes in and out;
The rheumy vault will force your eyes to weep,

---

0 s.d. 1 *Halberds* guards carrying halberds, a combination spear and battle-axe
1 *led* Qq. Some editors emend to 'lead'.
8 *try* Q1 (tyer Q2, tire Q3) test. Q3's reading, which results from modernising the
  spelling of the turned letters in Q2, makes less sense, given Christian belief about
  the inexhaustible mercy of God.
9 *yet from* even though it comes from
10 *sad* heavy
12–22 From Sylvester's translation of Du Bartas. See Appendix, 4.
14 *checkless* unchecked
17 *usherless* unannounced, without the ceremonious attendants to which you are
  accustomed in court
18 *rheumy* damp

Whilst you behold true desolation;
A rocky barrenness shall pierce your eyes,   20
Where all at once one reaches, where he stands,
With brows the roof, both walls with both his hands.

AURELIA

It is too good. Blessed spirit of my lord,
Oh, in what orb so e'er thy soul is throned,
Behold me worthily most miserable!   25
Oh, let the anguish of my contrite spirit
Entreat some reconciliation.
If not, oh joy, triumph in my just grief;
Death is the end of woes, and tears' relief.

PIETRO

Belike your lord not loved you, was unkind?   30

AURELIA

Oh heaven!
As the soul loves the body, so loved he;
'Twas death to him to part my presence,
Heaven to see me pleased.
Yet I, like to a wretch given o'er to hell,   35
Brake all the sacred rites of marriage
To clip a base, ungentle, faithless villain,
Oh God, a very pagan reprobate! –
What should I say? – Ungrateful, throws me out,
For whom I lost soul, body, fame, and honour.   40
But 'tis most fit: why should a better fate
Attend on any who forsake chaste sheets,
Fly the embrace of a devoted heart
(Joined by a solemn vow 'fore God and man)
To taste the brackish blood of beastly lust   45
In an adulterous touch? Oh ravenous immodesty,

---

20 *pierce* Q2–3 (pain Q1)

24 *orb* heavenly sphere

28 *oh joy, triumph* Q3 (O joy! triumph Q1–2). Hunter emends to 'O joy triumph'
    (i.e. oh enjoy your triumph), but perhaps Aurelia, like Juliet at *Measure for
    Measure* II.iii.35–6, both acknowledges her guilt and takes 'the same with joy'.

31–47 Compare *Hamlet* I.ii.140–152 and III.iv.54–93. In contrast to Gertrude,
    Aurelia's contrition is indicated by the fact that she herself invokes the
    unfavourable comparison between her husband and her adulterous lover.

32 *loves* ed. (lov'd Qq)

33 *part* part from

36 *Brake* Broke

38 *reprobate* rejected by God

45 *brackish* salty, lecherous

Insatiate impudence of appetite!
Look, here's your end: for mark, what sap in dust,
What sin in good, even so much love in lust.
Joy to thy ghost, sweet lord; pardon to me!   50
CELSO
'Tis the Duke's pleasure this night you rest in court.
AURELIA
Soul, lurk in shades; run shame from brightsome skies:
In night the blind man misseth not his eyes.

              Exit AURELIA, [FERRARDO, CELSO *and attendants*]

MALEVOLE
Do not weep, kind cuckold; take comfort man; thy betters
have been *beccos:* Agamemnon, emperor of all the merry   55
Greeks that tickled all the true Trojans, was a *cornuto;*
Prince Arthur, that cut off twelve kings' beards, was a *cor-*
nuto; Hercules, whose back bore up heaven and got forty
wenches with child in one night –
PIETRO
Nay, 'twas fifty.   60
MALEVOLE
Faith, forty's enough, o' conscience – yet was a *cornuto.*
Patience; mischief grows proud; be wise.
PIETRO
Thou pinchest too deep, art too keen upon me.
MALEVOLE
Tut, a pitiful surgeon makes a dangerous sore; I'll tent thee

---

47 *impudence* shamelessness
48 *here's your end* i.e. my sad situation is the conclusion to which such appetite
   comes
   sap moisture
51 *'Tis* Q3 (It is Q1–2)
53 From Sylvester's translation of Du Bartas (ed. Snyder, I, 354): 'While nights
   black muffler hoodeth up the skies, / The sillie blind-man misseth not his eyes:'
   (ll. 565–6).
57 *Prince Arthur ... beards* Nennius' *History of the Britons*, Chapter 50, reports
   that Arthur defeated the Saxon kings in twelve battles.
58–61 Hercules is reputed to have held up the sky while Atlas fetched the apples
   from the Garden of the Hesperides and to have impregnated the fifty daughters
   of Thespius in one night. His cuckolding, however, seems to be apocryphal.
62 *Patience ... wise* A variation of the advice offered to Celso in I.iv to 'temporise'
   or bide one's time, in this case until Mendoza's overconfidence grows.
64 *a pitiful ... sore* Proverbial (Tilley P 270), but perhaps inspired by *Il Pastor Fido*
   IV.v, where the priest Nicander characterises his interrogation of Amarillis in

to the ground. Thinkest I'll sustain myself by flattering thee   65
because thou art a prince? I had rather follow a drunkard
and live by licking up his vomit, than by servile flattery.

PIETRO

Yet great men ha' done't.

MALEVOLE

Great slaves fear better than love, born naturally for a coal-
basket, though the common usher of princes' presence,   70
Fortune, ha' blindly given them better place. I am vowed to
be thy affliction.

PIETRO

Prithee, be: I love much misery, and be thou some to me.

Enter BILIOSO

MALEVOLE

Because you are an usurping duke. (*To* BILIOSO) Your lordship's well returned from Florence.   75

BILIOSO

Well returned, I praise my horse.

MALEVOLE

What news from the Florentines?

BILIOSO

I will conceal the Great Duke's pleasure, only this was his
charge: his pleasure is that his daughter die, Duke Pietro be
banished for banishing his blood's dishonour, and that   80
Duke Altofront be reaccepted. This is all, but I hear Duke
Pietro is dead.

MALEVOLE

Ay, and Mendoza is Duke. What will you do?

BILIOSO

Is Mendoza strongest?

---

similar terms: 'if I have / Piers't with my wordes thy soule, like a Phisicion I /
Have done, who searcheth first the wound / Where it suspected is:' (sig. L4).
tent clean and probe a wound

69–70 *for a coal-basket* to carry coals, a dirty, low-status occupation

71 *ha'* Q1–2 (hath Q3)

73 *some* ed. (sonne Qq). Pietro's request that Malevole be a 'sonne' to him would
make sense if the latter also loved misery, rather than inflicting it, but it seems
more likely that the compositor misread a mss. 'm' for a double 'n' and that the
error was subsequently overlooked.

78 *Great Duke* The Medici Dukes of Florence were styled 'Grand Duke of Tuscany'.

80 *for banishing* i.e. for the purpose of banishing Aurelia's dishonour by removing
her husband from public office and the public eye

MALEVOLE
  Yet he is.   85
BILIOSO
  Then yet I'll hold with him.
MALEVOLE
  But if that Altofront should turn straight again?
BILIOSO
  Why, then I would turn straight again.
  'Tis good run still with him that has most might:
  I had rather stand with wrong, than fall with right.   90
MALEVOLE
  What religion will you be of now?
BILIOSO
  Of the Duke's religion, when I know what it is.
MALEVOLE
  Oh Hercules!
BILIOSO
  Hercules? Hercules was the son of Jupiter and Alcmena.
MALEVOLE
  Your lordship is a very wit-all.   95
BILIOSO
  Wit-all?
MALEVOLE
  Ay, all-wit.
BILIOSO
  Amphitrio was a cuckold.
MALEVOLE
  Your lordship sweats; your young lady will get you a cloth
  for your old worship's brows.   100

                                               Exit BILIOSO

Here's a fellow to be damned; this is his inviolable maxim,
'Flatter the greatest and oppress the least' – a whoreson
flesh-fly that still gnaws upon the lean, galled backs.

87 *turn straight* return promptly
91–98 Q2–3 (not in Q1). Q2 mistakenly repeats l. 90 again after the addition.
95 *wit-all* (i) a superior intellect (because he could identify Hercules' parents), and
     (ii) a wittol, in the double sense of complacent cuckold and fool
98 *Amphitrio ... cuckold* Apparently Malevole's pun has made Bilioso think of
     Alcmena's husband, Amphitryon, cuckolded by the god.
99 *a cloth* (i) to dry his forehead, and (ii) to hide his horns
101 *maxim* Maxims were specifically associated with 'politic' shrewdness in the
     Renaissance.
103 *flesh-fly* 'a type of the parasite, as in Jonson's Mosca' (Jackson and Neill)
     galled backs i.e. of those oppressed like beasts of burden whose saddles or yokes
     rub their flesh raw

PIETRO
Why dost then salute him?
MALEVOLE
Faith, as bawds go to church: for fashion sake. Come, be   105
not confounded; th' art but in danger to lose a dukedom.
Think this: this earth is the only grave and Golgotha
wherein all things that live must rot. 'Tis but the draught
wherein the heavenly bodies discharge their corruption, the
very muckhill on which the sublunary orbs cast their excre-   110
ments. Man is the slime of this dung-pit, and princes are the
governors of these men. For, for our souls, they are as free
as emperors', all of one piece; there goes but a pair of shears
betwixt an emperor and the son of a bagpiper; only the
dyeing, dressing, pressing, glossing makes the difference.   115
Now, what art thou like to lose? –
A gaoler's office to keep men in bonds,
Whilst toil and treason all life's good confounds.
PIETRO
I here renounce forever regency.
Oh Altofront, I wrong thee to supplant thy right,   120
To trip thy heels up with a devilish sleight,
For which I now from throne am thrown; world-tricks
    abjure,
For vengeance, though't comes slow, yet it comes sure.
Oh, I am changed, for here, 'fore the dread power,
In true contrition I do dedicate   125
My breath to solitary holiness,
My lips to prayer, and my breast's care shall be
Restoring Altofront to regency.

104 *salute* greet
105 *Faith* Q1–2 (I'faith Q3)
106 *th'* Q1–2 (thou Q3)
107 *Golgotha* the boneyard or 'place of skulls' where Jesus was executed according
     to Matthew xxvii.33
108–111 *the draught ... excrements* The earth, conceived of as being at the centre of
     the Ptolemaic universe, is compared to a 'draught' or privy because the area
     beneath the sphere of the moon was understood to be corrupt and decaying.
     Compare *Hamlet* II.ii.297–303.
113–14 *there goes ... bagpiper* Compare *Measure for Measure* I.ii.27–8.
115 *dressing, glossing* steps in the finishing of cloth
118 *confounds* overthrows, brings to nothing
122 *world-tricks abjure* 'I swear off worldly deceits'
124 *here, 'fore* ed. (heerefore Qq)

MALEVOLE
   Thy vows are heard, and we accept thy faith.

                  Undisguiseth himself

                 Enter FERNEZE *and* CELSO

   Altofront, Ferneze, Celso, Pietro –   130
   Banish amazement: come, we four must stand
   Full shock of Fortune; be not so wonder-stricken.
PIETRO
   Doth Ferneze live?
FERNEZE   For your pardon.
PIETRO
   Pardon and love. Give leave to recollect
   My thoughts dispersed in wild astonishment.   135
   My vows stand fixed in heaven, and from hence
   I crave all love and pardon.
MALEVOLE
   Who doubts of Providence,
   That sees this change, a hearty faith to all?
   He needs must rise who can no lower fall,   140
   For still impetuous vicissitude
   Touseth the world; then let no maze intrude
   Upon your spirits; wonder not I rise,
   For who can sink that close can temporise?
   The time grows ripe for action; I'll detect   145
   My privat'st plot, lest ignorance fear suspect.
   Let's close to counsel, leave the rest to fate:
   Mature discretion is the life of state.

                                            Exeunt

130 ed. Italicised in Qq as if a stage direction, but apparently meant to underscore
     the discovery of each of the three associates to Pietro.
131–3 ed. (prose in Qq)
134 *Give ... recollect* Permit me to collect
140 *who* Q1–2 (not in Q3)
142 *maze* amazement
145 *detect* reveal
147 *close to* meet privately for

Act V, Scene i

Enter BILIOSO *and* PASSARELLO

BILIOSO
Fool, how dost thou like my calf in a long stocking?

PASSARELLO
An excellent calf, my lord.

BILIOSO
This calf hath been a reveller this twenty year; when
Monsieur Gundi lay here ambassador, I could have carried
a lady up and down at arm's end in a platter, and I can tell   5
you there were those at that time, who, to try the strength
of a man's back and his arm, would be coistered. I have
measured calves with most of the palace, and they come
nothing near me; besides, I think there be not many
armours in the arsenal will fit me, especially for the head-   10
piece. I'll tell thee –

PASSARELLO
What, my lord?

BILIOSO
I can eat stewed broth as it comes seething off the fire, or a
custard as it comes reeking out of the oven, and I think
there are not many lords can do it. [*Smells his pomander*   15
ball] A good pomander, a little decayed in the scent, but six
grains of musk ground with rosewater and tempered with a
little civet shall fetch her again presently.

PASSARELLO
Oh ay, as a bawd with *aqua vitae*.

Act V, Scene i Addition 7, probably by Webster
   1 *long stocking* See the note to I.ii.6.
   4 *Monsieur Gundi* Jeromo de Gondi, Count de Retz, French Ambassador
     Extraordinary, came to England in 1578 to plead for Mary, Queen of Scots.
   7 *coistered* a nonce-word of uncertain meaning, possibly, as E. K. Deighton sug-
     gests (*The Old Dramatists: Conjectural Readings* [Westminster, 1896], p. 6), a
     misreading for 'hoistered', supported
10–11 *especially for the head-piece* Bilioso's boast about his head size is an ironic
     reminder of his cuckold's horns.
  14 *reeking* steaming
  15 *pomander* perfume ball, worn around the neck or carried
  18 *civet* a musky secretion obtained from the glands of a civet-cat
     fetch restore

BILIOSO
And what, dost thou rail upon the ladies as thou wert   20
wont?

PASSARELLO
I were better roast a live cat, and might do it with more
safety. I am as secret as thieves to their painting. There's
Maquerelle, oldest bawd and a perpetual beggar. Did you
never hear of her trick to be known in the City?   25

BILIOSO
Never.

PASSARELLO
Why, she gets all the picture-makers to draw her picture;
when they have done, she most courtly finds fault with
them one after another and never fetcheth them. They in
revenge of this execute her in pictures as they do in   30
Germany and hang her in their shops. By this means is she
better known to the stinkards than if she had been five
times carted.

BILIOSO
'Fore God, an excellent policy!

PASSARELLO
Are there any revels tonight, my lord?   35

BILIOSO
Yes.

PASSARELLO
Good my lord, give me leave to break a fellow's pate that
hath abused me.

BILIOSO
Whose pate?

PASSARELLO
Young Ferrard, my lord.   40

BILIOSO
Take heed, he's very valiant; I have known him fight eight
quarrels in five days, believe it.

PASSARELLO
Oh, is he so great a quarreller? Why then he's an arrant
coward.

BILIOSO
How prove you that?   45

---

23 *as thieves to* ed. (to thieves as Q3). A much emended passage, but Jackson and
   Neill's hypothesis of a simple transposition is plausible, and their reading rein-
   forces the idea of a conspiracy of silence.
32 *the stinkards* the rabble
33 *carted* displayed to the public in an open cart as punishment
42 *quarrels* duels

PASSARELLO
  Why thus: he that quarrels seeks to fight; and he that seeks
  to fight, seeks to die; and he that seeks to die, seeks never
  to fight more; and he that will quarrel and seeks means
  never to answer a man more, I think he's a coward.
BILIOSO
  Thou canst prove anything.   50
PASSARELLO
  Anything but a rich knave, for I can flatter no man.
BILIOSO
  Well, be not drunk, good fool; I shall see you anon in the
  presence.

                                                   Exeunt

[Act V, Scene ii]

Enter MALEVOLE *and* MAQUERELLE, *at several doors
opposite, singing*

MALEVOLE
  'The Dutchman for a drunkard,'
MAQUERELLE
  'The Dane for golden locks,'
MALEVOLE
  'The Irishman for usquebaugh,'
MAQUERELLE
  'The Frenchman for the (—).'
MALEVOLE
  Oh, thou art a blessed creature! Had I a modest woman to   5
  conceal, I would put her to thy custody, for no reasonable
  creature would ever suspect her to be in thy company. Ha,
  thou art a melodious Maquerelle, thou picture of a woman
  and substance of a beast!

                    Enter PASSARELLO

---

50 *prove* Bilioso means 'to justify by logic', but Passarello seems to take him to
   mean 'turn out to be'.
53 *Exeunt* ed. (Exit [Bilioso] Q3). Since Q3 has Passarello enter nine lines later, a
   new scene is indicated here.

 3 *usquebaugh* whisky
 4 *(—)* 'pox', but probably meant to be left unsung for comic effect
 8 *picture* because she is so heavily 'painted'
 9 s.d.–38 Addition 8, probably by Webster.

MAQUERELLE
  Oh fool, will ye be ready anon to go with me to the revels;   10
  the hall will be so pestered anon.
PASSARELLO
  Ay, as the country is with attorneys.
MALEVOLE
  What hast thou there, fool?
PASSARELLO
  Wine. I have learnt to drink since I went with my lord
  ambassador; I'll drink to the health of Madam Maquerelle.   15
MALEVOLE
  Why, thou wast wont to rail upon her.
PASSARELLO
  Ay, but since, I have borrowed money of her. I'll drink to
  her health now as gentlemen visit brokers or as knights
  send venison to the City: either to take up more money or
  to procure longer forbearance.   20
MALEVOLE
  Give me the bowl. I drink a health to Altofront, our
  deposed Duke. [Drinks]
PASSARELLO
  I'll take it so. [Drinks] Now I'll begin a health to Madam
  Maquerelle! [Drinks]
MALEVOLE
  Pew! I will not pledge her.   25
PASSARELLO
  Why, I pledged your lord.
MALEVOLE
  I care not.
PASSARELLO
  Not pledge Madam Maquerelle! Why then will I spew up
  your lord again with this fool's finger.
MALEVOLE
  Hold. I'll take it. [Drinks]   30
MAQUERELLE
  Now thou hast drunk my health, fool, I am friends with
  thee.

---

11 *pestered* crowded
17–20 ed. (I ... her/Ile ... brokers/Or ... Citty/Eather ... forbearance/ Q3)
18–19 *knights ... City* Because hunting rights were controlled by the great
    landowners, a gift of deer meat was an appropriate way for a knight to gain the
    favour of a merchant money-lender.
19 *take up* borrow
20 *to ... forbearance* to extend the date of repayment
29 *your lord* i.e. the wine he just drank

PASSARELLO

Art? Art?

When Griffon saw the reconciled quean,
Offering about his neck her arms to cast,   35
He threw off sword and heart's malignant stream,
And lovely her below the loins embraced.

Adieu, Madam Maquerelle.   *Exit*

MALEVOLE

And how dost thou think o' this transformation of state
now?   40

MAQUERELLE

Verily, very well, for we women always note, the falling of
the one is the rising of the other: some must be fat, some
must be lean; some must be fools, and some must be lords;
some must be knaves, and some must be officers; some
must be beggars, some must be knights; some must be cuck-   45
olds, and some must be citizens. As for example, I have two
court dogs, the most fawning curs, the one called Watch,
th'other Catch; now I, like Lady Fortune, sometimes love
this dog, sometimes raise that dog, sometimes favour
Watch, most commonly fancy Catch; now that dog which I   50
favour I feed, and he's so ravenous that what I give he never
chaws it, gulps it down whole, without any relish of what
he has but with a greedy expectation of what he shall have;
the other dog, now –

MALEVOLE

No more dog, sweet Maquerelle, no more dog. And what   55
hope hast thou of the Duchess Maria? Will she stoop to the
Duke's lure? Will she come, think'st?

34–7 R. E. R. Madelaine has pointed out (*NQ*, Dec. 1972) that this passage is a
parody of Richard Haydocke's translation of some lines from Ariosto's *Orlando
Furioso*: 'When Grifon sawe the reconciled King / Offring, about his necke his
armes to cast: / He cast off sworde, and harts malignant sting, / And lovely him
below the loynes embrac't'. Originally quoted as an example of decorous behaviour by an inferior to a superior, the embrace 'below the loins' acquires a bawdy
sense in Passarello's version.

39 *transformation of state* the fall of Duke Pietro

41–2 *we ... other* Women's experience with rising and falling in its sexual forms,
Maquerelle implies, makes them knowledgeable about the vicissitudes of
Fortune.

44 *officers* sergeants, whose job is to arrest knaves

45–6 *cuckolds ... citizens* A comic deflation of opposing categories, since the cuckolding of citizens by gentlemen was a stock joke in the private theatres.

47 *court dogs* presumably because of their skill at fawning or flattery

56–7 *stoop ... lure* like a trained hawk returning to the falconer's decoy

MAQUERELLE

Let me see, where's the sign now? Ha' ye e'er a calendar?
Where's the sign, trow you?

MALEVOLE

Sign? Why, is there any moment in that?   60

MAQUERELLE

Oh, believe me, a most secret power. Look ye, a Chaldean
or an Assyrian, I am sure 'twas a most sweet Jew told me,
court any woman in the right sign, you shall not miss; but
you must take her in the right vein then: as, when the sign
is in Pisces, a fishmonger's wife is very sociable; in Cancer,   65
a precisian's wife is very flexible; in Capricorn, a merchant's wife hardly holds out; in Libra, a lawyer's wife is
very tractable, especially if her husband be at the term; only
in Scorpio 'tis very dangerous meddling. Has the Duke sent
any jewel, any rich stones?   70

Enter CAPTAIN

MALEVOLE

Ay, I think those are the best signs to take a lady in. – By
your favour, signior, I must discourse with the Lady Maria,
Altofront's Duchess; I must enter for the Duke.

CAPTAIN

She here shall give you interview. I received the guardship
of this citadel from the good Altofront, and for his use I'll   75
keep it till I am of no use.

MALEVOLE

Wilt thou? Oh heavens, that a Christian should be found in
a buff jerkin! Captain Conscience, I love thee, captain. We
attend.

Exit CAPTAIN

And what hope hast thou of this Duchess' easiness?   80

MAQUERELLE

'Twill go hard. She was a cold creature ever; she hated

---

58 *the sign* the astrological sign

61–9 Marston's jokes turn on the associations between the signs of the zodiac and
the qualities of the husband: Puritans are 'crabbed'; merchants (those cuckolded
citizens) have horns like goats; the scales of justice make Libra the fit sign for
lawyers' wives, especially when their husbands are too busy at court sessions
('the term') to prevent their infidelity; the scorpion has a sting in its tail, possibly
an allusion to venereal disease.

77–8 *that a Christian ... buff jerkin* Soldiers did not have a great reputation for
piety at this time.

80 *easiness* persuadability

monkeys, fools, jesters, and gentlemen-ushers extremely;
she had the vile trick on't, not only to be truly modestly
honourable in her own conscience, but she would avoid the
least wanton carriage that might incur suspect, as, God   85
bless me, she had almost brought bed-pressing out of
fashion; I could scarce get a fine for the lease of a lady's
favour once in a fortnight.

MALEVOLE

Now, in the name of immodesty, how many maidenheads
hast thou brought to the block?   90

MAQUERELLE

Let me see – heaven forgive us our misdeeds! – Here's the
Duchess.

[Act V, Scene iii]

Enter MARIA *and* CAPTAIN

MALEVOLE

God bless thee, lady.

MARIA

Out of thy company.

MALEVOLE

We have brought thee tender of a husband.

MARIA

I hope I have one already.

MAQUERELLE

Nay, by mine honour, Madam, as good ha' ne'er a husband   5
as a banished husband; he's in another world now. I'll tell
ye, lady, I have heard of a sect that maintained when the
husband was asleep the wife might lawfully entertain
another man, for then her husband was as dead; much
more, when he is banished.   10

MARIA

Unhonest creature!

---

82 *monkeys* considered lustful; compare Othello's exclamation, 'Goats and mon-
    keys!' (IV.i.263)

85 *carriage* behaviour

87 *a fine* a fee

90 *brought ... block* sold

 3 *tender* offer

 7 *a sect* identified in John Taylor's *A Bawd* as the Puritan group, The Family of
    Love (*Works*, 1635, p. 102).

11 *Unhonest* Unchaste

MAQUERELLE

Pish! Honesty is but an art to seem so. Pray ye, what's honesty, what's constancy, but fables feigned, odd old fool's
chat, devised by jealous fools to wrong our liberty.

MALEVOLE

Molly, he that loves thee is a duke, Mendoza; he will main-   15
tain thee royally, love thee ardently, defend thee powerfully, marry thee sumptuously, and keep thee in despite of
Rosicleer or Donzel del Phoebo. There's jewels. [*Offering
them*] If thou wilt, so; if not, so.

MARIA

Captain, for God's sake save poor wretchedness   20
From tyranny of lustful insolence;
Enforce me in the deepest dungeon dwell
Rather than here; here round about is hell.
O my dear'st Altofront, where e'er thou breathe,
Let my soul sink into the shades beneath   25
Before I stain thine honour; this thou hast,
And long as I can die, I will live chaste.

MALEVOLE

'Gainst him that can enforce, how vain is strife?

MARIA

She that can be enforced has ne'er a knife.
She that through force her limbs with lust enrolls   30
Wants Cleopatra's asps and Portia's coals.
God amend you!

Exit with CAPTAIN

12–14 A combination of *Il Pastor Fido* III.v: 'This honesty is but an art to seem so'
(sig. H4); and I.iii: 'What's faith? what's constancy? but fables feigned / By jealous men?' (sig. C3).

15 *Molly* familiar form of 'Maria'

18 *Rosicleer . . . Phoebo* heroes of the popular romance *Mirror of Knighthood* translated from the Spanish of Diego Ortunez de Calahorra

20 *sake* Q3 (love Q1–2)

22–7 Adapted from Seneca, *Hercules Furens* 419–21, where the tyrant Lycus
attempts to force Megara, the wife of Hercules, to marry him to secure his rule.

26 *this* Q3 ('tis Q1–2)

29 A variant of *Hercules Furens* 426, 'Who can be forced has not learned how to
die', but influenced by the story of Lucrece, who stabbed herself after being
raped.

31 *Cleopatra's . . . coals* Cleopatra and Portia both defied ill fortune by committing
suicide, using poisonous snakes and swallowing coals, respectively. See
Shakespeare's *Julius Caesar* IV.iii.152–6 and *Antony and Cleopatra* V.ii.

MALEVOLE

Now the fear of the Devil for ever go with thee!
Maquerelle, I tell thee, I have found an honest woman.
Faith, I perceive when all is done, there is of women, as of   35
all other things, some good, most bad; some saints, some
sinners; for as nowadays no courtier but has his mistress,
no captain but has his cockatrice, no cuckold but has his
horns, and no fool but has his feather, even so no woman
but has her weakness and feather too, no sex but has his –   40
I can hunt the letter no farther. [*Aside*] Oh God, how loathsome this toying is to me, that a duke should be forced to
fool it! Well, *stultorum plena sunt omnia*; better play the
fool lord, than be the fool lord. – Now, where's your
sleights, Madam Maquerelle?   45

MAQUERELLE

Why, are ye ignorant that 'tis said, a squeamish affected
niceness is natural to women and that the excuse of their
yielding is only, forsooth, the difficult obtaining. You must
put her to't; women are flax and will fire in a moment.

MALEVOLE

Why, was the flax put into thy mouth, and yet thou – thou   50
set fire? Thou inflame her?

MAQUERELLE

Marry, but I'll tell ye now, you were too hot.

MALEVOLE

The fitter to have inflamed the flaxwoman.

MAQUERELLE

You were too boisterous, spleeny; for indeed –

MALEVOLE

Go, go. Thou art a weak panderess, now I see.   55
Sooner earth's fire heaven itself shall waste,
Than all with heat can melt a mind that's chaste.
Go, thou the Duke's lime-twig, I'll make the Duke turn thee
out of thine office. What, not get one touch of hope, and
had her at such advantage!   60

---

38 *cockatrice* whore
41 *hunt the letter* keep up the alliteration
43 *stultorum ... omnia* 'All places are full of fools' (Cicero, *Epistolae ad Familiares*
     IX.xxii.4), also used as the motto for Marston's *The Scourge of Villainie*, Satire
     X.
47 *niceness* coyness
50–1 your inflammatory words had little success provoking her desires, didn't they?
54 *spleeny* impetuous, violent in approach
58 *lime-twig* branch smeared with sticky bird-lime to snare birds

MAQUERELLE

Now, o' my conscience, now I think in my discretion, we
did not take her in the right sign; the blood was not in the
true vein, sure.   *Exit*

Enter BILIOSO

BILIOSO

Make way there! The Duke returns from the enthronement.
– Malevole –   65

MALEVOLE

'Out, rogue!'

BILIOSO

Malevole –

MALEVOLE

'Hence, ye gross-jawed, peasantly – out, go!'

BILIOSO

Nay, sweet Malevole, since my return, I hear you are
become the thing I always prophesied would be: an   70
advanced virtue, a worthily-employed faithfulness, a man
o' grace, dear friend. Come – what? *Si quoties peccant
homines* ... If as often as courtiers play the knaves, honest
men should be angry – why, look ye, we must collogue
sometimes, forswear sometimes.   75

MALEVOLE

Be damned sometimes.

BILIOSO

Right. *Nemo omnibus horis sapit.* No man can be honest at
all hours. Necessity often depraves virtue.

MALEVOLE

I will commend thee to the Duke.

BILIOSO

Do let us be friends, man.   80

MALEVOLE

And knaves, man.

---

63 s.d.–94 Addition 9, probably by Marston.

66, 68 echoing Bilioso's words to him at II.iii.30, 34

71 *advanced virtue* a virtuous man who has gained favour

72–3 *Si ... homines* 'If as often as men sinned'. From Ovid, *Tristia* II.33–4, where
   Ovid pleads for mercy from Caesar by arguing that even Jupiter does not send
   his thunderbolts every time man sins. Bilioso's plea that courtiers must be knaves
   gains ironic approval from Malevole.

74 *collogue* speak deceitfully

77 *Nemo ... sapit* Adapted from Pliny, *Naturalis Historia* VII.xli.2 and translated
   by Bilioso, who changes 'be wise' (*sapit*) to 'be honest'.

BILIOSO
Right. Let us prosper and purchase; our lordships shall live
and our knavery be forgotten.

MALEVOLE
He that by any ways gets riches, his means never shames
him.   85

BILIOSO
True.

MALEVOLE
For impudency and faithlessness are the mainstays to greatness.

BILIOSO
By the Lord, thou art a profound lad.

MALEVOLE
By the Lord, thou art a perfect knave. Out, ye ancient   90
damnation!

BILIOSO
Peace, peace! And thou wilt not be a friend to me as I am a
knave, be not a knave to me as I am thy friend and disclose
me. Peace, cornets.

[Act V, Scene iv]

Enter PREPASSO *and* FERRARDO, *two pages with lights,*
CELSO *and* EQUATO, MENDOZA *in duke's robes, and*
GUERRINO

MENDOZA
On, on; leave us, leave us.

Exeunt all saving MALEVOLE

Stay, where is the hermit?

MALEVOLE
With Duke Pietro, with Duke Pietro.

MENDOZA
Is he dead? Is he poisoned?

MALEVOLE
Dead as the Duke is.   5

MENDOZA
Good, excellent; he will not blab, secureness lives in
secrecy; come hither, come hither.

---

82 *purchase* acquire possessions and, as a consequence, titles

0 s.d. 2–3 *and* GUERRINO ed. (BILIOSO *and* GUERRINO Q1–3)
1 s.d. placed before l. 1 in Qq
    saving except

MALEVOLE
  Thou hast a certain strong villainous scent about thee my
  nature cannot endure.

MENDOZA
  Scent, man? What returns Maria? What answer to our suit?   10

MALEVOLE
  Cold, frosty; she is obstinate.

MENDOZA
  Then she's but dead; 'tis resolute, she dies:
  Black deed only through black deed safely flies.

MALEVOLE
  Pew! *Per scelera semper sceleribus tutum est iter.*

MENDOZA
  What, art a scholar? Art a politician? Sure thou art an   15
  arrant knave.

MALEVOLE
  Who I? I have been twice an under-sheriff, man. Well, I will
  go rail upon some great man, that I may purchase the *basti-*
  nado, or else go marry some rich Genoan lady and instantly
  go travel.   20

MENDOZA
  Travel when thou art married?

MALEVOLE
  Ay, 'tis your young lord's fashion to do so, though he was
  so lazy being a bachelor that he would never travel so far

---

12   *resolute* resolved
13   *deed safely* ed. (deeds safely Q1–2; deed, safely Q3)
14   *Per ... iter* Malevole supplies the Latin original of Mendoza's maxim from
     Seneca *Agammemnon* 115, where it is spoken by the murderous Clytemnestra.
17   *under-sheriff* Hunter compares Harrington, *Metamorphosis of Ajax,* (ed.
     Donno): 'The saying is, "Thrice an undersheriff and ever a knave"' (p. 206).
17–30   *Well ... Puritan* Addition 10, probably by Webster and introduced in Q3 by
     the following lines, perhaps representing an alternative beginning meant to
     replace ll. 1–11:

                    Enter MALEVOLE *and* MENDOZA

     MENDOZA
        Hast been with Maria?
     MALEVOLE
        As your scrivener to your usurer. I have dealt about taking of this commodity,
        but she's cold, frosty.

     The joke in ll. 24–30 is reminiscent of *Hamlet* V.i.148–55, but the addition awk-
     wardly interrupts Mendoza's questioning of Malevole.
18–19   *bastinado* beating

as the university, yet when he married her, tails off, and
'Catso, for England'.   25
MENDOZA
And why for England?
MALEVOLE
Because there is no brothel-houses there.
MENDOZA
Nor courtesans?
MALEVOLE
Neither: your whore went down with the stews, and your
punk came up with your Puritan.   30
MENDOZA
Canst thou empoison? Canst thou empoison?
MALEVOLE
Excellently, no Jew, 'pothecary, or politician better. Look
ye, here's a box; whom wouldst thou empoison? Here's a
box [*Giving it*] which opened, and the fume taken up in
conduits through which the brain purges itself, doth   35
instantly for twelve hours' space bind up all show of life in
a deep senseless sleep. Here's another [*Giving it*] which,
being opened under the sleeper's nose, chokes all the power
of life, kills him suddenly.
MENDOZA
I'll try experiments; 'tis good not to be deceived. – So, so,   40
catso!

Seems to poison MALEVOLE

Who would fear that may destroy?
Death hath no teeth nor tongue,
And he that's great, to him are slaves,
Shame, Murder, Fame, and Wrong.   45
Celso!

Enter CELSO

24 *tails off* turns tail
29–30 *your whore ... Puritan* Another attack on Puritan hypocrisy. The licensed
brothels in Southwark were shut down in 1546 as a consequence of the
Reformation, but prostitutes returned with the new label 'punks'.
32 *no Jew ... better* A manifestation of the pervasive anti-Semitism responsible for
the myth of Jews as poisoners. Compare Marlowe's *The Jew of Malta*.
35 *conduits* Q1–2, Q3 corrected (commodites Q3 uncorrected) the nostrils
42–3 ed. (Who ... tong/ Qq)
43 *Death ... tongue* i.e. Dead men don't speak
    nor Q1–2 (or Q3)
46 s.d. ed. (at l. 39 in Qq, repeated at l. 45 in Q2)

CELSO
  My honoured lord?
MENDOZA
  The good Malevole, that plain-tongued man,
  Alas, is dead on sudden wondrous strangely;
  He held in our esteem good place.   50
  Celso, see him buried, see him buried.
CELSO
  I shall observe ye.
MENDOZA
  And Celso, prithee let it be thy care tonight
  To have some pretty show to solemnise
  Our high installment, some music, masquery.   55
  We'll give fair entertain unto Maria,
  The Duchess to the banished Altofront;
  Thou shalt conduct her from the citadel
  Unto the palace; think on some masquery.
CELSO
  Of what shape, sweet lord?   60
MENDOZA
  What shape? Why, any quick-done fiction,
  As some brave spirits of the Genoan dukes
  To come out of Elysium, forsooth,
  Led in by Mercury, to gratulate
  Our happy fortune –   65
  Some such anything, some far-fet trick,

48–51 ed. (prose in Qq)
52 *observe* obey
55 *high installment* coronation
   masquery The court masque involved the entry of masked dancers and musi-
   cians, introduced by a 'presenter' who explained their identity and the fictional
   reason for their appearance – usually to pay some compliment to the presiding
   monarch and his queen. The dancers performed for the assembled company and
   then 'took out' men or women (depending on the sex of the dancers) from the
   audience to dance with them before their departure.
61 *What* ed. (Why Qq)
   fiction trisyllabic
63 *Elysium* the Islands of the Blessed, where those favoured by the gods enjoy a
   pleasant afterlife
64 *Mercury* who conducted the souls of the dead to the underworld
   gratulate express joy at
65–8 ed. (prose in Qq)
66–7 *far-fet ... ladies* 'Far-fet and dear-bought is good for ladies' was a proverbial
   (and prejudicial) complaint about ladies' taste for expensive imports. See Tilley,
   D 12.

Good for ladies, some stale toy or other,
No matter so't be of our devising.
Do thou prepar't, 'tis but for fashion sake;
Fear not, it shall be graced, man; it shall take.   70

CELSO
All service.

MENDOZA
All thanks.
Our hand shall not be close to thee. Farewell.
[*Aside*] Now is my treachery secure, nor can we fall;
Mischief that prospers men do virtue call.   75
I'll trust no man; he that by tricks gets wreaths
Keeps them with steel: no man securely breathes.
Out of distuned ranks the crowd will mutter, 'Fool';
Who cannot bear with spite, he cannot rule.
The chiefest secret for a man of state   80
Is to live senseless of a strengthless hate.   *Exit*

MALEVOLE (*Starts up and speaks*)
Death of the damned thief! I'll make one i' the masque;
thou shalt ha' some brave spirits of the antique dukes.

CELSO
My lord, what strange delusion!

MALEVOLE
Most happy, dear Celso; poisoned with an empty box! I'll   85
give thee all anon. My lady comes to court, there is a whirl

69 *fashion* Q1 (a fashion Q2–3)

70 *graced* applauded

72–3 ed. (All … farewell/ Qq)

73 *close* closed, tight-fisted

75 Translating Seneca, *Hercules Furens* 251–2, where it describes the temporary tri-
    umph of Lycus, ultimately killed by Hercules.

76 *wreaths* crowns

77 *steel* the sword, violence

78 *distuned* Q1 (deserved Q2–3). Hunter and Jackson and Neill run on the previous
    line ('No man securely breathes / Out of deserved ranks'), but this overrides the
    comma after 'breathes' in the quartos and undercuts Mendoza's ruthlessness.
    'Distuned', moreover, fits both with Marston's consistent devaluation of the mob
    and with his imagery of harmony and disharmony.

79 Adapted from Seneca, *Phoenissae* 654, where it expresses the sentiments of the
    tyrant Eteocles, warned by Jocasta in the next speech that 'hated sovereignty is
    never long retained'.

80–1 Adapted from Seneca, *Hercules Furens* 353, where it is spoken by Lycus.

81 *senseless of* indifferent to
    s.d. Q1–2 (not in Q3)

82–3 ed. (Death … some/Brave … Dukes/ Qq)

of fate comes tumbling on, the castle's captain stands for
me, the people pray for me, and the great leader of the just
stands for me. Then courage, Celso –
For no disastrous chance can ever move him   90
That feareth nothing but a God above him.

Exeunt

[Act V, Scene v]

Enter PREPASSO *and* BILIOSO, *two pages, before them*
MAQUERELLE, BIANCA, *and* EMILIA

BILIOSO
Make room there, room for the ladies! Why gentlemen, will
not ye suffer the ladies to be entered in the great chamber?
Why gallants! And you sir, to drop your torch where the
beauties must sit, too!
PREPASSO
And there's a great fellow plays the knave. Why dost not   5
strike him?
BILIOSO
Let him play the knave, i' God's name. Thinkest thou I have
no more wit than to strike a great fellow? The music! More

---

91 *feareth* ed. (leaveth Qq). Hunter compares the idea of lines 90–1 with Psalm
   xxvii.1 ('The Lord is my light and my salvation; whom shall I fear?') and the
   Senecan proverb 'The safest thing is to fear nothing except God'. Given such parallels and the similarities between *f* and *l*, *v* and medial *r* in Elizabethan hand-
   writing, an emendation seems appropriate.
91 s.d. Q1 (not in Q2–3)

Act V, Scene v Part of Scene iv in Qq, but the clear stage indicates a scene break
   2 *the great chamber* The stage now represents the hall in the Genoan palace where
     the masque is staged. Marston captures the sense of disorderly pushing and shov-
     ing characteristic of such occasions as Bilioso, carrying a chamberlain's staff,
     speaks to persons who, in some cases, may only be glimpsed in the stage door-
     way or imagined to be outside it.
   3 *drop your torch* let the pitch from your torch drop
   8–9 *More lights! Revelling! Scaffolds!* (more lights, revelling, scaffolds, Qq).
     Editors since Bullen have compounded the latter two into 'revelling-scaffolds',
     perhaps on the assumption that there is no need for Bilioso to call for revels, but
     I find no evidence that this term was used in the period. 'Scaffolds' are probably
     the risers on which the spectators at the masque sit, here assembled before the
     theatre audience's eyes.

lights! Revelling! Scaffolds! Do you hear? Let there be oaths
enough ready at the door; swear out the Devil himself. Let's   10
leave the ladies, and go see if the lords be ready for them.

All save the ladies depart

MAQUERELLE
And by my troth, beauties, why do you not put you into the
fashion? This is a stale cut; you must come in fashion. Look
ye, you must be all felt, felt and feather, a felt upon your
bare hair. Look ye, these tiring things are justly out of   15
request now. And – do ye hear? – you must wear falling
bands, you must come into the falling fashion; there is such
a deal o' pinning these ruffs, when the fine clean fall is
worth all; and again, if you should chance to take a nap in
the afternoon, your falling band requires no poting stick to   20
recover his form. Believe me, no fashion to the falling, I say.

BIANCA
And is not Signior St. Andrew Jaques a gallant fellow now?

MAQUERELLE
By my maidenhead, la, honour and he agrees as well
together as a satin suit and woollen stockings.

EMILIA
But is not Marshall Make-room, my servant in reversion, a   25
proper gentleman?

MAQUERELLE
Yes, in reversion as he had his office, as in truth he hath all
things in reversion: he has his mistress in reversion, his
clothes in reversion, his wit in reversion, and indeed is a
suitor to me for my dog in reversion. But in good verity, la,   30
he is as proper a gentleman in reversion as – and indeed, as

9–10 *oaths enough* 'to chase the gate-crashers away' (Hunter)

14 *felt and feather* a felt hat decorated with feathers

15 *bare hair* Q2–3 (head Q1)

tiring things head-dresses or tiaras of wire or net

16–17 *falling bands* linen collars, so-called because they turned down over the
shoulders, as opposed to the starched ruff, which circled the neck and stood out
straight. See Linthicum, *Costume in the Drama of Shakespeare*, pp. 155–61.

20 *poting stick* or poking stick, used to form the loops on a ruff

21 *the falling* with a bawdy innuendo

22 *Signior St. Andrew Jaques* Q1 (Signior St. Andrew Q2–3). A hit at James' Scots
followers, perhaps altered to avoid direct offence to the King

25 *in reversion* next in line, at second-hand. Sovereigns besieged for offices, like
court ladies for favours, placed candidates on a waiting-list and granted the right
to succeed in turn.

fine a man as may be, having a red beard and a pair of
warped legs.

BIANCA

But i' faith, I am most monstrously in love with Count
Quidlibet-in-Quodlibet; is he not a pretty, dapper, wimble   35
gallant?

MAQUERELLE

He is even one of the most busy-fingered lords; he will put
the beauties to the squeak most hideously.

[Enter BILIOSO]

BILIOSO

Room! Make a lane there! The Duke is entering. Stand
handsomely, for beauty's sake; take up the ladies there! So,   40
cornets, cornets!

[Act V, Scene vi]

Enter PREPASSO, [*who*] *joins to* BILIOSO, *two pages
with lights,* FERRARDO, MENDOZA, *at the other door
two pages with lights, and the* CAPTAIN *leading in*
MARIA, *the Duke* [MENDOZA] *meets* MARIA, *and
closeth with her; the rest fall back*

MENDOZA

Madam, with gentle ear receive my suit;
A kingdom's safety should o'er-peise slight rites;
Marriage is merely Nature's policy.
Then since, unless our royal beds be joined,
Danger and civil tumult frights the state,   5
Be wise as you are fair, give way to fate.

32–3 *red ... legs* Possibly a touch of self-satire, since Jonson had ridiculed the little
legs of Crispinus-Marston in *Poetaster* II.i.77.
   warped Q1–2 (wrapped Q3)
35 *Quidlibet-in-Quodlibet* 'Which-you-will in What-you-will'. A 'quodlibet' was
   also a term for a university disputation at this time; see *OED* 1.
   wimble ed. (windle Q1, un-idle Q2–3) active, nimble; a term also used in
   Antonio and Mellida III.ii.188

0 s.d. 2 *with lights* Q1–2 (and lights Q3)
1–7 Adapted from Lycus' courtship of Megara in *Hercules Furens* 360–1, 413,
   358. Echoes of Seneca continue in Maria's defiance of Mendoza's death threats.
2 *o'er-peise ... rites* outweigh the mere ceremony of marriage vows
3 *policy* stratagem, trick (*OED* 4b)

MARIA

What wouldst thou, thou affliction to our house?
Thou ever-devil, 'twas thou that banished'st
My truly noble lord.

MENDOZA

I? 10

MARIA

Ay, by thy plots, by thy black stratagems,
Twelve moons have suffered change since I beheld
The lovèd presence of my dearest lord.
Oh thou far worse than death! He parts but soul
From a weak body; but thou, soul from soul 15
Dissever'st, that which God's own hand did knit.
Thou scant of honour, full of devilish wit!

MENDOZA

We'll check your too intemperate lavishness;
I can and will.

MARIA

What canst? 20

MENDOZA

Go to, in banishment thy husband dies.

MARIA

He ever is at home that's ever wise.

MENDOZA

You'st never meet more; reason should love control.

MARIA

Not meet?
She that dear loves, her love's still in her soul. 25

MENDOZA

You are but a woman, lady; you must yield.

MARIA

Oh save me, thou innated bashfulness,
Thou only ornament of woman's modesty!

MENDOZA

Modesty! Death, I'll torment thee!

MARIA

Do; urge all torments, all afflictions try; 30
I'll die my lord's as long as I can die.

---

17 *scant of* lacking in
22 A classical commonplace, derived from Ovid's *Fasti* I.493 and Cicero, *Tusculan Disputations* V.xxxvii.108. Compare *Antonio's Revenge* (ed. Hunter), II.i.163.
23 *You'st* You must
28 *woman's* Q1, 3 (womens' Q2)

MENDOZA
  Thou obstinate, thou shalt die. – Captain, that lady's life
  Is forfeited to justice. We have examined her,
  And we do find she hath empoisonèd
  The reverend hermit; therefore we command   35
  Severest custody. Nay, if you'll do's no good,
  You'st do's no harm; a tyrant's peace is blood.
MARIA
  Oh, thou art merciful, oh gracious devil!
  Rather by much let me condemnèd be
  For seeming murder, than be damned for thee!   40
  I'll mourn no more; come, girt my brows with flowers,
  Revel and dance; soul, now thy wish thou hast;
  Die like a bride; poor heart, thou shalt die chaste.

                Enter AURELIA *in mourning habit*

AURELIA
  'Life is a frost of cold felicity,
  And death the thaw of all our vanity.'   45
  Was't not an honest priest that wrote so?
MENDOZA
  Who let her in?
BILIOSO   Forbear.
PREPASSO   Forbear.
AURELIA
  Alas, calamity is everywhere.
  Sad misery, despite your double doors,
  Will enter even in court.   50
BILIOSO
  Peace!
AURELIA
  I ha' done. One word: take heed! I ha' done.

                Enter MERCURY *with loud music*

32–3 ed. (prose in Qq)
33 *forfeited* Q1–2 (fortified Q3)
40 *for thee* i.e. for marrying thee
41–2 *flowers,/Revel and dance; soul,* Q2–3 (flowers/Revel and dance, soul, Q1).
    Most editors have followed Bullen in placing a semi-colon after 'flowers', making
    Maria urge her soul, rather than the courtiers, to revel, but this seems unwar-
    ranted.
44 Assigned to Maria in Q1, Aurelia in Q2–3.
44–5 From an epigram in *Chrestoleros* (1598) by the cleric Thomas Bastard, a
    friend of Marston's from his Middle Temple days.

MERCURY
Cyllenian Mercury, the god of ghosts,
From gloomy shades that spread the lower coasts,
Calls four high-famèd Genoan dukes to come   55
And make this presence their Elysium;
To pass away this high triumphal night
With song and dances, court's more soft delight.

AURELIA
Are you god of ghosts? I have a suit depending in hell
betwixt me and my conscience; I would fain have thee help   60
me to an advocate.

BILIOSO
Mercury shall be your lawyer, lady.

AURELIA
Nay, faith, Mercury has too good a face to be a right
lawyer.

PREPASSO
Peace, forbear! Mercury presents the masque.   65

*Cornets: the song to the cornets, which playing, the
masque enters:* MALEVOLE, PIETRO, FERNEZE, *and*
CELSO *in white robes, with duke's crowns upon laurel
wreaths, pistolets and short swords under their robes.*

MENDOZA
Celso, Celso, court Maria for our love. – Lady, be gracious,
yet grace.

MALEVOLE *takes his wife to dance*

MARIA
With me, sir?
MALEVOLE   Yes, more lovèd than my breath;
With you I'll dance.
MARIA   Why then you dance with death.
But come, sir, I was ne'er more apt for mirth.   70

---

53 *Cyllenian* Mercury was supposedly born on Mt. Cyllene
54 *coasts* regions
59 *depending* pending
62 *Mercury ... lawyer* Mercury was the god of eloquence and patron of lawyers
63 *right* genuine
65 s.d. 2 *enters*: Q2–3 (enters. Enter Q1)
    s.d. 4 *pistolets* pistols
66 Harris suggests that Mendoza mistakes the disguised Malevole for Celso.
    court Q1–2 (count Q3)
70 *for* Q1–2 (to Q3)

Death gives eternity a glorious birth;
Oh, to die honoured, who would fear to die?
MALEVOLE
They die in fear who live in villainy.
MENDOZA
Yes, believe him, lady, and be ruled by him.

PIETRO *takes his wife* AURELIA *to dance*

PIETRO
  Madam, with me?
AURELIA   Wouldst then be miserable?   75
PIETRO
  I need not wish.
AURELIA
  Oh yet forbear my hand; away, fly, fly!
  Oh seek not her that only seeks to die.
PIETRO
  Poor lovèd soul!
AURELIA   What, wouldst court misery?
PIETRO
  Yes.
AURELIA She'll come too soon. Oh my grieved heart!   80
PIETRO
  Lady, ha' done, ha' done.
  Come, let's dance; be once from sorrow free.
AURELIA
  Art a sad man?
PIETRO   Yes, sweet.
AURELIA   Then we'll agree.

FERNEZE *takes* MAQUERELLE, *and* CELSO, BIANCA; *then*
the cornets sound the measure; one change, and rest

FERNEZE [*To* BIANCA]
  Believe it, lady; shall I swear? Let me enjoy you in private,
  and I'll marry you, by my soul.   85

---

71 *birth* ed. (breath Qq). An emendation would seem indicated here by the pattern
    of rhyming couplets established in ll. 68–9 and 72–3 and by the death–birth con-
    trast, which makes more sense than 'glorious breath'. The compositor might be
    inclined to err since he had just set 'breath' at the end of l. 68.
72–3 Compare Florio, *First Fruites*, quoting Guevara: 'It is far better to dye with
    honour, then to live with shame. A Roman proverb' (fol. 93v).
82 *Come*, Q2–3 (Come down Q1)
83 s.d. 2 *change* round, figure, often accompanied by a change of partners, which
    does not seem to occur here

BIANCA
I had rather you would swear by your body; I think that
would prove the more regarded oath with you.

FERNEZE
I'll swear by them both to please you.

BIANCA
Oh damn them not both to please me, for God's sake.

FERNEZE
Faith, sweet creature, let me enjoy you tonight, and I'll   90
marry you tomorrow fortnight, by my troth, la.

MAQUERELLE
On his troth, la, believe him not; that kind of cony-catching
is as stale as Sir Oliver Anchovy's perfumed jerkin. Promise
of matrimony by a young gallant to bring a virgin lady into
a fool's paradise, make her a great woman, and then cast   95
her off – 'tis as common, as natural to a courtier as jealousy
to a citizen, gluttony to a Puritan, wisdom to an alderman,
pride to a tailor, or an empty handbasket to one of these
sixpenny damnations. Of his troth, la, believe him not –
traps to catch polecats!   100

MALEVOLE (*To* MARIA)
Keep your face constant. Let no sudden passion speak in
your eyes.

MARIA
Oh my Altofront!

PIETRO (*To* AURELIA)
A tyrant's jealousies
Are very nimble; you receive it all.   105

AURELIA
My heart, though not my knees, doth humbly fall

---

89 *damn them not* by swearing an oath you won't keep
92 *cony-catching* cheating
95 *a great woman* (i) a titled lady (ii) pregnant
96–7 *as jealousy ... Puritan* Contemporary comedy regularly depicted citizens as
      anxious cuckolds and Puritans as hypocritical gluttons.
98 *handbasket* carried by common streetwalkers, the 'sixpenny damnations' whom
      Maquerelle scorns as inferior competition to the courtly assignations she
      arranges
100 *polecats* prostitutes
104 s.d. Q1 (not in Q2–3, which mark Aurelia's reply 'To Pietro')
104–5 As Malevole has just done, Pietro apparently reveals his identity to his part-
      ner here, probably by partly removing his mask. His statement may mean either
      that Aurelia has suffered from his jealousy or that Mendoza is easily suspicious.
      Hunter, preferring the latter, glosses 'receive' as 'understand' (*OED* 7) and
      makes the last clause a question.

Low as the earth to thee.

MALEVOLE   Peace! Next change. No words.

MARIA
Speech to such? Ay, oh what will affords!

Cornets sound the measure over again, which danced,
they unmask

MENDOZA
Malevole?

They environ MENDOZA, *bending their pistols on him*

MALEVOLE [*Removing his disguise*]
No.   110

MENDOZA
Altofront! Duke Pietro! Ferneze! – Hah!

ALL
Duke Altofront! Duke Altofront!

Cornets, a flourish

MENDOZA
Are we surprised? What strange delusions mock
Our senses? Do I dream? Or have I dreamt
This two days' space? Where am I?   115

They seize upon MENDOZA

MALEVOLE
Where an arch-villain is.

MENDOZA
Oh, lend me breath till I am fit to die!
For peace with Heaven, for your own soul's sake,
Vouchsafe me life!

PIETRO
Ignoble villain, whom neither Heaven nor Hell,   120
Goodness of God or man, could once make good.

MALEVOLE
Base treacherous wretch, what grace canst thou expect,
That hast grown impudent in gracelessness?

MENDOZA
Oh, life!

---

107 *MALEVOLE* Assigned to Pietro in Qq. I follow Dyce, Bullen and Hunter in assuming that it is Malevole who speaks to Maria and directs the action of the masquers.
108 *to such?* i.e. who would speak to such as Mendoza?
115 *two days' space* his time as Duke
117 *breath* Q2–3 (breath to live Q1)

MALEVOLE

Slave, take thy life.   125
Wert thou defenced, through blood and wounds,
The sternest horror of a civil fight,
Would I achieve thee, but prostrate at my feet,
I scorn to hurt thee: *'tis the heart of slaves*
That deigns to triumph over peasants' graves.   130
For such thou art, since birth doth ne'er enroll
A man 'mong monarchs, but a glorious soul.
Oh, I have seen strange accidents of state:
The flatterer, like the ivy, clip the oak
And waste it to the heart; lust so confirmed   135
That the black act of sin itself not shamed
To be termed courtship.
Oh, they that are as great as be their sins,
Let them remember that th'inconstant people
Love many princes merely for their faces   140
And outward shows, and they do covet more
To have a sight of these than of their virtues.
Yet thus much let the great ones still conceit,
When they observe not Heaven's imposed conditions,
They are no kings, but forfeit their commissions.   145

MAQUERELLE

Oh good my lord, I have lived in the court this twenty year;
they that have been old courtiers and come to live in the

126 *defenced, through* ed. (defenced through Qq)
    defenced defended (by troops or fortifications)
128 *achieve* succeed in killing
128–9 *prostrate ... thee* Harris compares Guicciardini, *Maxims* 72, Series C (trans.
    Domandi): 'There is nothing in life more desirable or more glorious than to see
    your enemy prostrate on the ground and at your mercy. And this glory is dou-
    bled if you use it well, that is, by showing mercy and being content to have won'
    (Harper Torchbooks, p. 60).
129 *I ... thee* italicised in Q1–3
131–2 *since ... soul* a humanist commonplace. See Michael McCanles, *Jonsonian
    Discriminations: The Humanist Poet and the Praise of True Nobility* (1992), pp.
    46–65.
133–54 Addition 11, probably by Marston. The references to 'princes' and 'kings' in
    ll. 140 and 145 have been altered in some copies to 'men', probably as the result
    of censorship, for the doctrine that kings lose the right to rule when they lack
    virtue would have seemed threatening to Jacobean authorities.
136–7 *That ... courtship* That adultery is shamelessly called courtliness
143 *conceit* ed. (conceal Q3) have in mind, conceive (*OED* 3). Hunter's emendation,
    positing the confusion of 'conceal' for 'conceate', makes good sense here, while
    Q3 does not.

City, they are spighted at and thrust to the walls like apricots, good my lord.

BILIOSO

My lord, I did know your lordship in this disguise; you   150
heard me ever say if Altofront did return I would stand for
him. Besides, 'twas your lordship's pleasure to call me wit-
toll and cuckold; you must not think, but that I knew you,
I would have put it up so patiently.

MALEVOLE (*To* PIETRO *and* AURELIA)
You o'er-joyed spirits, wipe your long-wet eyes.   155

(*Kicks out* MENDOZA)

Hence with this man! An eagle takes not flies.
(*To* PIETRO *and* AURELIA)
You to your vows.
(*To* MAQUERELLE) And thou unto the suburbs.
(*To* BILIOSO)
You to my worst friend I would hardly give;
Thou art a perfect old knave, all pleasèd live.
(*To* CELSO *and the* CAPTAIN, [*embracing them*])
You two unto my breast.
(*To* MARIA, [*embracing her*]) Thou to my heart.   160
The rest of idle actors idly part.
And as for me, I here assume my right,
To which I hope all's pleased. To all, goodnight!

Cornets, a flourish

Exeunt omnes

FINIS

148–9 *thrust ... apricots* pushed aside, as apricots are trained to grow against walls
where the reflected heat will ripen them (Hunter)

150–4 Hypocritical self-justification after the fact, like that of Falstaff in *1 Henry IV*
II.iv.267–270

155 s.p. ed. (omitted in Q3, where the additions interrupt Malevole's speech)
o'er-joyed Q2–3 (are joyed Q1)

157–63 Altofronto's rapid disposition of the other characters to their fortunes is reminiscent of Jaques' valedictions at *As You Like It*, V.iv.186–93.

157 *your vows* (i) marriage vows (ii) resolution to live a retired life of contemplation
(see IV.v.125–8)
the suburbs where brothels were located

159 *all pleasèd live.* Q2–3 (live, Q1) although may you be pleased to live. Many editors seize on the ambiguity of Q1 to emend to 'All-pleasèd, live', making these
words an affirmation of the Captain, Celso, and Maria.

161 Q2–3 (not in Q1)
idle trifling, unimportant
idly carelessly

EPILOGUE

Your modest silence, full of heedy stillness,
Makes me thus speak: a voluntary illness
Is merely 'scuseless; but unwilling error,
Such as proceeds from too-rash, youthful fervour,
May well be called a fault, but not a sin: 5
Rivers take name from founts where they begin.
   Then let not too severe an eye peruse
The slighter breaks of our reformèd Muse,
Who could herself herself of faults detect,
But that she knows 'tis easy to correct,   10
Though some men's labour; troth, to err is fit,
As long as wisdom's not professed, but wit.
Then till another's happier Muse appears,
Till his Thalia feast your learned ears,
To whose desertful lamps pleased Fates impart   15
Art above Nature, Judgement above Art,
   Receive this piece, which hope nor fear yet daunteth;
   He that knows most, knows most how much he wanteth.

Epilogue ed. (Epilogus Q2–3)
  1 *heedy* attentive
  2 *illness* wrong-doing
  3 *'scuseless* Q2 (senseless Q3)
  6 *Rivers ... begin* i.e. one must judge things by their origins (and intentions)
  8 *breaks* errors
    our reformèd Muse now freer from the affected diction ridiculed by Jonson in *Poetaster* V.iii.
10–11 *'tis ... labour* it is easy to criticise, though some men work hard at it
13–14 *till ... ears* till the more fortunate comic genius of another produces a comedy fit for your educated taste. The reference is probably to Ben Jonson, to whom Marston dedicates the play.
 15 *desertful lamps* well-deserving powers of illumination
 16 A double tribute to Jonson, both echoing the last line of the prologue to *Cynthia's Revels* and applauding the emphasis on judicious revision central to his Horatian aesthetic.
 18 Typical of Marston's modest self-presentation to his audience. Compare the prologues to *Antonio and Mellida* and *Antonio's Revenge*.

131

APPENDIX

Illustrations of Marston's Borrowing

1
I.vi.79–92
(a) Lines 79–80, from Florio, *First Fruites* (1578), fol. 90v, translating Guevara's *Dial of Princes*:

> I say moreover, that yll women are woorse, then the infernall Furies, for in Hell the badde are onely tormented, but the unruly women doo tormente both good and badde.

(b) Lines 86–8, from Florio, *First Fruites*, fol. 91, translating Guevara:

> Women are hastye in askyng, determined in woorkynge, impacient in sufferynge, extreme in desiringe: for I see certayne women that wyl set them selves to desyre such thynges as was never seene of the dead, neyther heard of the livyng.

(c) Lines 89–92, from the Satyr's condemnation of Corisca in Guarini, *Il Pastor Fido*, trans. by Dymock (1602) (sig. D2v–D3):

> Oh womans treacherie! that is the cause
> That hath begotten love this infamy.
> How ever love be in his nature good,
> With them his goodnesse suddenly he leeseth.
> They never suffer him to touch their hearts,
> But in their faces onely build his bowre.
> * * *
> What is it that they use, which is not counterfeit?
> Ope they their mouthes? they lie: moove they their eyes?
> They counterfeit their lookes: If so they sigh,
> Their sighes dissembled are. In summe, each act,
> Each look, each gesture, is a very lie.
> Nor is this yet the worst. 'Tis their delight,
> Them to deceive ev'n most, that trust them most;
> And love them least, that are most worthy love.
> * * *
> Lovers beleeve me, women once ador'd,
> Are worser then the griesly powers of hell.

2

II.iv.35–49, from Corisca's advice to Amarillis in *Il Pastor Fido*
III.v (sigs. H4–H4v):

> This life's too short
> To pass it over with one onely love:
> Men are too sparing of their favours now,
> (Whether't be for want, or else for frowardnesse)
> The fresher that we are, the dearer still:
> Beautie and youth once gone w'are like Bee hives
> That hath no honey, no nor yet no waxe.
> Let men prate on they do not feele our woes,
> For their condition differs much from ours,
> The elder that they grow, they grow the perfecter:
> If they loose beautie, yet they wisedome gaine:
> But when our beautie fades that oftentimes
> Conquers their greatest witts, strait fadeth all our good,
> There cannot be a vilder thing to see
> Then an old woman. Therfore ere thou age attaine,
> Know me thy selfe, and use it as thou shouldst.

3

III.ii.2–14, from 'The First Day of the First Weeke' of Joshua
Sylvester's translation of *The Divine Weeks and Works of
Guillaume de Saluste Sieur Du Bartas*, ed. Susan Snyder, 2 vols.
(Oxford, 1979), I, 126–7 (by permission of Oxford University
Press):

> The Night is she that all our travailes eases,
> Buries our cares, and all our griefes appeases:
> The Night is she that with her sable wing
> In gloomie Darknes hushing every thing,
> Through all the World dumb silence doth distill,
> And wearied bones with quiet sleepe doth fill.
>   * * *
> He that still stooping, toughes (i.e. tugs) against the tide
> His laden Barge alongst a Rivers side,
> And filling shoares with shoutes, doth melt him quite,
> Upon his pallet resteth yet at Night.
> He that in Sommer, in extreamest heat
> Scorched all-day in his owne scalding sweat
> Shaves with keene Sythe, the glory and delight
> Of motly Medowes, resteth yet at Night,
> And in the armes of his deere Pheere forgoes
> All former troubles and all former woes.
> Onely the learned Sisters sacred Minions,
> While silent Night under her sable pinions

Foldes all the World; with paine-less paine they tread
A sacred path that to the Heav'ns doth lead;
And higher then the Heav'ns their Readers raise
Upon the wings of their immortall Layes.
   Even now I listned for the Clocke to Chime
Dayes latest hower, that for a little time
The Night might ease my Labours; but I see
As yet *Aurora* hath scarce smil'd on mee:
My Worke still growes;   (ll. 545–50, 567–87)

4

IV.v.12–22, from Du Bartas, 'The Handy-Crafts', *The Divine
Weeks*, I, 382–3:

   Who ful of wealth and Honours blandishment,
Among great Lords his younger yeeres hath spent;
And quaffing deeply of the *Courte*-delights,
Us'd nought but Tilts, Turneis, and Masks, and Sights:
If in his age, his Princes angrie doombe
With deepe disgrace drive him to live at home
In homely Cottage, where continually
The bitter smoake exhales aboundantlie
From his before-un-sorrow-drained braine
The brackish vapours of a silver rayne:
Where usher-les, both day and night the *North,
South, East, and West* windes, enter and go forth:
Where round-about the low-rooft broken wals
In steed of Arras hang with Spiders caules:
Where all at once he reacheth as he stands,
With browes the Roofe, both wals with both his hands:
He weeps, and sighes, and shunning Comforts aye,
Wisheth pale death a thousand times aday: (ll. 67–84)